Building Bridges
of Peaceful Coexistence between
Christians and Muslims
in Nigeria

Theodore Tochukwu Nnorom

ISBN: 978-1-9994478-0-9

Toronto, Canada

Dedicated to:

Mama Mary Pope

Contents

Acknowledgement v
Foreword...vii
General Introduction 1
Chapter One: Ethnic and Religious Complexitiesin Nigeria
....9
   1.1. Introduction...9
   1.2. The Historical Background of Nigeria....................9
   1.3. Islam in Nigeria..10
   1.4. Christianity in Nigeria..19
   1.5. The Contemporary Challenges to Christian-Muslim
       Coexistence in Nigeria.....................................24
   1.6. ....The Prerequisites for Effective Interreligious
       Dialogue in Nigeria 30
      1.6.1. Religious Freedom 30
      1.6.2. Openness 33
      1.6.3. Respect, Humility and Love 34
      1.6.4. Commitment...36
   1.7. Conclusion 37
Chapter Two: Making the Case for Theological Inclusivism
....38
   2.1. Introduction...38
   2.2. Exclusivism...44
   2.3. Pluralism 54
   2.4. Inclusivism..66
   2.5. Conclusion 79
Chapter Three: Comparing Inclusivism in
Christianity and Islam...80
   3.1. Introduction...80
   3.2. Gavin D'Costa: Trinitarian Theology
       and the Religions 81
      3.2.1. Trinitarian Christology 83

3.2.2. Trinitarian Pneumatology..............................85
3.2.3. Trinitarian Ecclesiology 86
3.3. Jacques Dupuis: Trinitarian Theology
    and Inclusive Pluralism 90
3.3.1. Christ in the Trinity 91
3.3.2. De Facto and De Jure of Religious Pluralism
   95
3.3.3. Ways of Salvation 97
3.4. Evaluation of Modern Inclusivism and
    Interreligious Dialogue 101
3.5. Islam and Inclusivism 108
3.6. Amir Hussain: From Tolerance to Dialogue........108
3.6.1. The People of the Book (ahk al-kitab) 109
3.6.2. Jesus as the Focal Point for Dialogue 110
3.7. Reza Shah-Kazemi: The Qur'an and Inclusivism 111
3.7.1. The Qur'an and the Spirit of Tolerance.......112
3.8. Evaluation of Inclusivism in Islam 117
3.9. Conclusion 120
Chapter Four: The Proposition of Dialogue of Life and
Action in the Nigerian Context.................................123
4.1. Introduction..123
4.2. Forms of Interreligious Dialogue and the Nigerian
    Experience...123
4.3. Dialogue of Theological Exchange.....................124
4.4. Dialogue of Religious Experience 128
4.5. Social Dialogues 131
4.5.1. Dialogue of Life..133
4.5.2. Dialogue of Action......................................141
4.6 Concluding Recommendations 147
General Conclusion...150
Bibliography 156

Acknowledgement

My utmost reverence goes to the almighty God by whose grace and mercy the opportunity to engage in this academic research was made possible.

I acknowledge and immensely appreciate the inspiring efforts of my supervisor Prof. Thomas Reynolds, who kindly accepted to undertake the task of supervising this work and the writing of the foreword. His patient guidance and encouragement through the course of this work was invaluable.

I would like to thank Prof. Darren Dias and Prof Mohammed Ovey for serving on my committee, for the insightful scrutiny and constructive criticisms that helped form my ideas.

My special appreciation goes to My Superior General, Very Rev. Dr. George Okorie and his Council of the Sons of Mary Mother of Mercy Congregation, and the entire brothers, especially my brothers in Canada Region. Your support was a huge source of encouragement.

I am grateful to the bishop of the Catholic Diocese of Peterborough, His Excellency, Most Rev. Daniel Miehm, the priests and the faithful, especially my parishioners at St. Patrick's Kearney and the Church of the Holy Spirit, Burk's Falls, Ontario.

I am indebted to Mama Mary Pope for her love, care and support in ensuring that this work of dialogue could reach many people of our time.

I won't forget the invaluable and insightful suggestions of my good friends; Rev. Dr. Idara Out MSP and Rev. Barr. Paul Njoku SMMM. Thank you for the strength your support provided.

My friends Peter and Helga Finikar worked tirelessly on the setting, design and publication of this work. Thank you for your love, friendship and support.

My special thanks go to Mrs. Susan AdaoraOkpala who painstakingly edited this work. To my family and friends and everyone who in anyway helped in the production of this work, I sincerely appreciate all your help.

Foreword

In a time of urgent need for constructive Muslim-Christian relations in Nigeria, Theodore Nnorom's book is a well-conceived and solidly researched step forward. It advocates for an *inclusivist* approach to dialogue, building on positive resources from both Christian and Muslim perspectives. The topic is especially important given the current social and political context of Nigeria, where ongoing violence is often religiously motivated. The book develops an astute analysis of the historical and political roots of the conflict, carefully avoiding facile judgments about "religious" causes for violence, which can too quickly cast blame and cause further suspicion between religions. While the thesis is written from a Roman Catholic Christian point of view and argues for a theological position from sources rooted in Vatican II perspectives, it also respects and accounts for constructive possibilities for dialogue from within Muslim traditions. This strength provides a strong practical rationale for inclusivism in Nigeria in form of the dialogue of life and action.

It gives me great pleasure to write the foreword for this book. I was Theodore Nnorom's supervisor for Theology Master's thesis at St. Michael's College (in the Toronto School of Theology at the University of Toronto). Hence, I came to know the project well as it developed through various drafts; and I appreciated the dedication and commitment the author showed to its vision. His background experience, with family roots in Nigeria, and ordained ministry in the Church gives the writing a particular kind of authenticity and relevance.

The main themes of the discussion emerge clearly through the chapters, and display a sound analysis of significant scholars and authors in the field. I am especially impressed by the author's use of *both* Christian and Muslim authors representative of inclusivism, and how this, in turn, opens up practical applications for dialogue and cooperative relationships between religions. Indeed, the book makes a good case for inclusivism as the most reasonable position from within each tradition, allowing both for commitment to the truth and saving power of one's own tradition as well as for dialogical openness to others. Even if one disagrees with the analyses in places, this book can be a helpful resource for promoting interreligious dialogue in Nigerian contexts. It strongly supports further dialogue and peace-making initiatives. I am glad to commend this book and hope the author continues writing in this important topic.

Thomas E Reynolds
Vice Principal and Associate Professor of Theology
Emmanuel College, at Victoria University of the
University of Toronto and in the Toronto School of
Theology

General Introduction

Christianity and Islam are the two largest theistic and Abrahamic religions in the world, with their collective followership making up sixty percent of the world's population. Interactions between Christians and Muslims have existed since the seventh centuries. In the present-day post-modern society their members are drawn further to live side by side in communities owing to globalization.[1] Although this factor has profoundly improved their knowledge of each other, Christian-Muslim relations continues to be marred by spiteful confrontation and ferocious wars.[2] The prevalence of religiously motivated violence by Christians and Muslims is an increasing source of terror, insecurity, economic hardship and pertinent issue of global concern. The September 11, 2001 terrorist attacks in the United States of America, the November 18, 2015 attacks in Paris, and the attack in Brussels on March 22, 2016 represent a miniscule of the waves of terror carried out by radical Islamic groups. In a similar vein, the history

---

[1] Social and economic factors (and advances in technology) such as media technology, the internet, ease of travel and migration have facilitated contacts and encounters between peoples, cultures and languages. These factors have seemly compressed time and distance between peoples. It has aided in creating pluralistic societies. What used to be traditional and homogeneous societies have increasingly become intercultural societies. See. Fraxis X. Clooney, *Comparative Theology: Deep Learning across Religious Borders* (Maiden, MA: Wiley-Blackwell, 2010), 10.

[2] Catholic Church, "Declaration on the Relation of the Church to non-Christian Religion" -*Nostra Aetate,*http://www.vatican.va/archive/hist_councils/ii_vatican_council/documents/vat-ii_decl_19651028_nostra-aetate_en.html (accessed July 10, 2017), no. 3.

of Christianity is fraught with specific cases of violence against Islam. For example, the crusades, the inquisition and colonial conquests.[3] In addition, the rise of militant right-wing extremist groups in Europe and North America has increased the rate of religious violence in the recent years.[4] These events are symptomatic of the precarious situation of today's world in the face of the religious conflicts between these two major religions.

Presently, Nigeria is among the countries of the world mostly affected by religiously motivated violence. In the past two decades, religious violence between Christians and Muslims in Nigeria has escalated to unprecedented proportions. The emergence of Boko Haram with their numerous terrorist activities has brought notoriety to Nigeria within the global community.[5] The menace and scourge of the situation has raised some crucial theological

---

[3]M.D. Litonjua, "Religious Zealotry and Political Violence in Christianity and Islam," in *International Review of Modern Sociology*35, no.2 (2009), 307.

[4] Daniel Koehler, "Right-Wing Extremism and Terrorism in Europe: Current Development and Issues for the Future," in *Prism: A Journal of the Center for Complex Operations* 6, no.2 (2016), 84.

[5] Boko Haram is an Islamic extremist sect that has operated in Borno, Bauchi, Kano, Maiduguri, Abuja, Katsina and Yobe States, Nigeria. The sect began in the mid-1990s from a youth group at the Alhaji Muhammadu Ndimi mosque (an Ahlus Sunna Mosque) in Maiduguri. Its official name is; Jama'att Ahlis Sunna Lidda'awl-Jihad, an Arabic name, which means "People Committed to the Propagation of the Prophet's Teachings and Jihad. It follows the spirituality of the Iraqi scholar and spiritual leader, Ibn Taymiyyah. The first leader was Muhammad Yusuf(29 January 1970 – 30 July 2009). Their agenda is to purify Islam in Nigeria, reject westernization, and Islamize entire Nigeria. See. John Azumah, "Boko Haram in Retrospect," *Islam and Christian- Muslim Relations* 26, no.1 (2015), 39-40.

questions for the leaders of both religions: How can these two religions co-exist peacefully? Are there elements in Islam and Christianity that could form a common working ground for peaceful co-existence? What are the common religious values for fostering interreligious dialogue for adherents of both religions in the Nigerian context? How can this be realized?

There have been varied responses in Nigeria to the prevailing situation of religious conflicts between Christians and Muslims by pastors, imams, lay faithful and theologians alike. This kind of situation is not, however, peculiar to Nigeria, people all over the world have their dispositions to the presence of other religion. From the Christian perspective, many typologies have emerged in theology of religions that denote approaches to other faith traditions. One of the dominant paradigms to shape theological discourse is Alan Race's threefold paradigm.[6]

This paradigm categorizes Christian attitudes to other religions into exclusivism, pluralism and inclusivism. According to Race, exclusivism "counts the revelation in Jesus Christ as the sole criterion by which all religions including Christianity can be understood and evaluated."[7] Inclusivism "proceeds on the basis of commitment to two equally binding convictions: the universal will of God to save, and the uniqueness of revelation in Christ."[8] Finally, Race suggests that pluralism "seeks tolerance among

---

[6]Darren J. Dias, "Fifty Years and the Learning: Development in the Roman Catholic Church's Encounter with Religions," *Toronto Journal of Theology* 32, no.2 (2016), 354.

[7] Alan Race, Christians and Religious Pluralism (Maryknoll, New York: Orbis Books, 1982)11.

[8] Ibid., 54.

religions on the basis that our knowledge of God is partial in all faiths, including the Christians. Religion must acknowledge their need of each other if the full truth about God is to be available to mankind."[9]

This book appropriates inclusivism as a suitable paradigm for laying the theological foundation for building the bridges of peaceful coexistence between Christians and Muslims in Nigeria. This involves interpreting categories of theological inclusivism in Christianity and analogously relating them to Islamic categories. This approach adopts the understanding of hermeneutics in interreligious dialogue as defined by Catherine Cornille as "a category of convenience, invoked to cover a wide variety of critical issues in the area of interreligious understanding and interpretation." As well, "It may be used to refer both to theory and to the practice of interreligious understanding, and from any religious, cultural, or philosophical perspective."[10]Cornille further lists some of the approaches applied in this hermeneutical exercise: (i) the hermeneutical retrieval of resources for dialogue within one's own tradition, (ii) the pursuit of proper understanding of the other, (iii) the appropriation and reinterpretation of the other within one's own religious framework, and (iv) the borrowing of hermeneutical principles of another religion.[11]

While this book draws from these interrelated approaches, it will mainly apply the hermeneutical retrieval of resources for dialogue from within Christianity in pursuit

---

[9] Ibid., 72.

[10] Catherine Cornille, "Introduction: On Hermeneutics in dialogue," in *Interreligious Hermeneutics,* eds. Catherine Cornille and Christopher Conway (Eugene, Oregon: Cascade Books, 2010), ix.

[11] Ibid.

of dialogical engagement with Islam. This intra-dialogical approach offers theological principles from the matrix of Christian tradition as the basis for effective interreligious dialogue. At a secondary level, this work will also explore Islamic inclusivist positions as analogous to themes in Christian inclusivism and as a means to build dialogical bridge with Islam. The importance and suitability of inclusivism is its openness to other religions and firm commitment to ones' religion. David Cheetham elucidates:

> This is about finding the narrative resources within one's own religious tradition and about how one might view oneself viewing other religions. So, from Christian religious tradition, knowing the relational God of love allows one to see others as God sees them; as made in his image and love from eternity, as part of God's plan of salvation.[12]

Drawing from Cheetham's description, this book explores the teachings of the Second Vatican Council and selected Post-Conciliar documents to establish that inclusivism is a viable approach to Christian relations toward other religions.

Furthermore, I will explore the works of two prominent Catholic thinkers, Gavin D'Costa and Jacques Dupuis, who through their analysis of Trinitarian theology, developed pneumatological theologies that embrace the activities of the Spirit in other religions as theological grounds for dialogical engagement. To avoid the misinterpretation of this approach as an *a priori* imposition of Christian beliefs

---

[12]David Cheetham, "Inclusivisms: Honouring Faithfulness and Openness," in *Christians Approaches to other Faiths*, eds Alan Race and Paul M. Hedges (London:SCM, 2008), 78.

on Islam, this book investigates the works of two Muslim thinkers, Amir Hussein and Reza Shah-Kazemi, to identify analogous categories from the Islamic traditions for inclusive dialogical engagement with Christianity. Since the teaching on love of God and neighbor is a value shared by both religions, it forms an inclusive ground for dialogue. Therefore, this work argues that the application of love of God and neighbor will be more effective in the dialogue of life and action to facilitate peaceful co-existence between Nigerian Christians and Muslims.

The reality of interreligious conflicts between Christians and Muslims is a global phenomenon of epic proportion; however, this work focuses specifically on achieving its set goals using Nigeria as a case study. It seeks to provide Christians with a better understanding of Islam and its tenets, and in a way that supports peaceful co-existence between Christians and Muslims in Nigeria. This will help lay the foundation for mutual respect between Christians and Muslims in communities and enhance collaborative efforts towards development, justice and peace projects in Nigeria.

This book is a revised form of my master's degree thesis in the University of Toronto. I choose Nigeria because it is my home country and I have experienced the devastating consequences of interreligious conflict first hand. Therefore, this work offers a renewed insight into the hermeneutics of theological inclusivism for interreligious dialogue and collaboration between Muslims and Christians in Nigeria. Also, this book aims at promoting further theological conversation and investigation in the Christian-Muslim relationship in Nigeria.

Structurally, this book consists of four chapters including the introduction and the conclusion. The first chapter presents a brief historical background of the formation of Nigeria as a nation with emphasis on the advent and propagation of Islam and Christianity. It will describe the *modus operandi* of the various Islamic and Christian sects and their impacts on interreligious dialogue. Then, it explores the prerequisites for effective interreligious dialogue in contemporary Nigeria.

Chapter two examines the typologies in interreligious dialogue. This involves the analysis of Alan Race's threefold paradigm namely pluralism, exclusivism and inclusivism. I will examine each paradigm, while engaging the theologies of some proponent thinkers. Under the subsection discussing exclusivism, the views of theologians such as Karl Barth, Hendrick Kraemer and Emil Brunner will be briefly analyzed. Similarly, the analysis of pluralism will include a brief exploration of John Hick's and Paul Knitter's theological stance. The concept of inclusivism will be discussed alongside, Conciliar and Post-Conciliar theology, including the theologies of Pope Paul VI and Pope John Paul II.

The third chapter interprets in a synchronic comparative analysis the concepts of inclusivism in Christianity through the theoretical lenses of Gavin D'Costa and Jacques Dupuis, and Amir Hussein and Reza Shah-Kazemi in Islam. This will involve the examination of analogous positions of inclusivism in both religions as basis for pragmatic interreligious dialogue.

The fourth chapter explores the application of the four forms of interreligious dialogue in the Nigerian context. They include; dialogue of theological exchange, dialogue of religious experience, dialogue of life and dialogue of action. This chapter proposes that social dialogues, specifically the dialogue of life and action will be the most practical and effective dialogues in Nigerian context, because it bring into praxis Christian and Muslim inclusive categories of love of God and love of neighbor. This will be followed by the general conclusion, which summarizes and recaps the major themes of this work.

Chapter One

Ethnic and Religious Complexities in Nigeria

1.1. Introduction

This chapter briefly examines the history of the Nigeria nationhood, the advent of Islam and Christianity, and the challenges to the peaceful coexistence of both religions in Nigeria. It also highlights the prerequisites for pro-active Christian-Muslim relations in Nigerian. The goal of this chapter is to appraise the context and establish the challenges, which necessitates the application of theological inclusivist approach in Christian-Muslim relations in Nigeria

1.2. The Historical Background of Nigeria

Nigeria has a long history of human habitation dating to 500 B.C.[13] Prior to colonialism it was inhabited by multiple ethnicities of diverse cultures and languages, and the relationships between these groups was marked by intermarriage, trade and occasional warfare.

The early European explorers of Nigeria were entrepreneurs who established trade with the different ethnic groups but overtime these entrepreneurs leveraged their military strength to colonize the people.[14] Subsequently, in the late nineteenth century, the colonialists divided the people of the land into two protectorates (northern and southern) for administrative convenience; by 1914 effected the amalgamation of the two

---

[13] Toyin Falola, *The History of Nigeria* (Westport, London: Greenwood Press, 1999), 1.

[14] Toyin Falola, *Colonialism and Violence in Nigeria* (Bloomington and Indianapolis, IN: University Press, 2009), 1 - 2.

as a crown colony. Nigeria gained independence from Britain in 1960.

Since its independence, Nigeria has not been able to attain national cohesion, which could be blamed partly on the faulty and lopsided foundation laid by the British colonial administration and partly on other socio-political issues, which we shall highlight in this section. Nigeria, however, is richly blessed with both human and natural resources. It is home to 200 ethnic groups and over 250 languages. With a population of approximately one hundred and seventy-five million people, it is the most populous African nation and has the world's eighth largest population.[15] While these factors hold great potentials for Nigeria's advancement, the challenges of harnessing them and the incessant ethnic and religious crisis have remained insurmountable. The next section provides a brief overview of the history of Islam and Christianity in Nigeria to illuminate the nature of these ethnic and religious conflicts.

1.3. Islam in Nigeria

The first encounter between Islam and Northern Nigeria can been traced back to the early eleventh century through trans-Saharan trade.[16] The Arab and the Berber missionaries and traders are historically responsible for the introduction of Islam to the Kanem-Bornu Kingdom via the eastern route and to the other parts of the southern Sahara.[17]

---

[15] Ngozi Okonjo Iweala, *Reforming the Unreformable: Lessons from Nigeria* (Cambridge, MA: MIT Press, 2012), 1.

[16] Yushau Sodiq, "Muslim Perception of Christians and Christianity in Nigeria," in *Fractured Spectrum; Perspectives on Christian-Muslim Encounter in Nigeria*, ed. Akintunde E. Akinade (New York: Peter Lang Publishing Inc., 2013), 149.

Some notable Kanem-Bornu kings of this era like Ali Ghaji (1472-1504) and Idris Alooma (1571-1603) showed their commitment to Islam by their pilgrimage to Mecca.[18] The Kanem-Bornu kingdom was subsequently conquered by colonialists, and was divided among the British, French and Germans in 1900. This kingdom is part of the present-day Republic of Niger, Chad, Cameroun, and Nigeria.[19]

It is worth noting that Fulani nomads from Sudan, via trans-Sahara trade, played a significant role in the advent of Islam in Northern Nigeria. They settled comfortably with the Hausa tribe of Northern Nigeria and brought with them their religion. In this early stage, the encounter between Islam and Northern Nigerians was peaceful; however, towards the end of the 18th century, Islamic revival took place in most parts of West Africa. Around 1804 conflict erupted among the Muslims in the North of Nigeria. A Fulani Islamic scholar and reformist Sheik Usman dan Fodio (1754-1817) accused the Muslim leaders of mingling with the observances of heathendom, and sought to restore the lost purity and prestige of Islam and to establish a renewed model of Islamic piety and an Islamic caliphate under sharia law.[20] Between 1804-1808, he waged a jihad, which saw the defeat of many Hausa and Fulani city-states

---

[17] H.A. Drake, "Intolerance, Religious Violence, and Political Legitimacy in Late Antiquity," *Journal of American Academy of Religion* 79, no.1 (March 2011), 197.

[18] Marinus Iwuchkwu, *Muslim-Christian Dialogue in Postcolonial Northern Nigeria: The Challenges of Inclusive Cultural and Religious Pluralism* (New York: Palgrave Macmillan, 2013), 2.

[19] Ibid.

[20] Akintunde Akinade, *Christian Response to Islam in Nigeria: A Contextual Study of Ambivalent Encounters* (New York: Palgrave Macmillan, 2014), 4.

under the old Kanem-Bornu kingdom, and established an Islamic caliphate with the capital in Sokoto.[21] Akintunde Akinade, who has written extensively on Muslim-Christian relations in Nigeria, captures this jihad and its effects:

> The nineteenth-century jihad led by Usman dan Fodio led to the creation of the Sokoto caliphate and the consolidation of Islam in the region. Extending as far as Western Sudan, the Caliphate became the centralized authority in this region through its administrative, judicial and fiscal institutions. The Caliphate also provided the engine for religio-cultural homogenization in this region. Indigenous people were assimilated into Caliphate through its massive expansionist campaign. In the nineteenth century, the caliphate was for all intents and purposes, the largest empire in Africa, south of Sahara. The main driving ethos for this grandiose Islamic Empire was jihad, carried out to convert all the surrounding ethnic groups to Islam and establish Islamic practices and a policy that made Islamic sharia law the basis and core of social organization.[22]

The jihad of Fodio was the greatest propelling factor for the vast expansion and proliferation of Islam, across Northern Nigeria, the Middle Belt and some parts of Southwestern Nigeria.[23] Although the jihad was initiated to

---

[21]Thomas Walker Arnold, *The Preaching of Islam; A History of the Propagation of the Muslim Faith* (London: Luzac & Company, 1935), 327.

[22] Ibid., 39.

[23] T.A. Oladimeji, "The Spread of Islam in Nigeria: the case of Ijebuland," in *Selected Themes in the Study of Religions in Nigeria*, eds. S.G.A. Onibere and M.P.Adogbo (Lagos, Nigeria: Malthouse,

purify Islam of idol worship, somewhere along the line, it turned into a political and economic gambit. Some of the communities that practiced traditional religious worship were allowed to exist because of the money accrued from their taxation or *jiyza*. For non-Muslim communities, experiences of injustice, oppression, war, violence and slavery characterized the Caliphate era, and this remains the prism through which non-Muslims still continue to view Islam in Nigeria.[24] The Sokoto caliphate reigned for over one hundred years, and collapsed in 1903 under the military might of the British colonialists. Fodio's reformative jihad and intellectual reformation is very influential in the ideological structuring of contemporary Islamic religion in Nigeria. It accounts to why a considerable number of emergent radical Islamic groups contain a vestige of Fodio's *jihadic* mantra of reformation.[25]

2010), 106 - 107.

[24] Mathew Hassan Kukah and Kathleen McGarvey, "Christian-Muslim Dialogue in Nigeria: Social Political and theological Dimensions," in *Fractured Spectrum; Perspectives on Christian-Muslim Encounter in Nigeria*, ed. Akintunde E. Akinade (New York: Peter Lang Publishing Inc., 2013), 15.

[25] In an open letter to the governor of Kano State, Rabui Musa Kwankwaso, after an attack in Kano in 2011, the leader of the *Boko Haram* wrote: The reason [for our attack] are clear: 1. The Nigerian Government is a Kufur [infidel] system serving BOTH UNITED NATION (UN) AND CHRISTIAN ASSOCIATION OF NIGERIA (CAN). 2. We the Jama'atu Ahlisunnah Lidda'awati Wal-Jihad are MUSLIMS and are from the NORTHERN part of the country who spent eight years agitating for ISLAMIC STATE, STRIVING TO BRING BACK THE LOST GLORY OF UTHMAN DANFODIO. WHAT IS WRONG WITH THAT? Is just to go back to the ways of our creator (ALLAH) where justice, discipline, good morals, love and care, peace and progress etc. will prevail [sic]. See, *Sahara Reporters*,

The Muslims in Nigeria are divided into different sects, dominant among which are the Sufi, the Salafist and the Shia. The two Sufi brotherhoods are the Tijaniyya and the Qadiriyya. The two are essentially distinct and critical of each other even to the point of violent confrontation. The Qadiriyya was founded in Baghdad by ShekhAbdl al-Qadir al-Jaylani in the twelfth-century. It spread to North Africa and from there to Nigeria. It is the oldest Sufis brotherhood in Nigeria. Usman dan Fodio was a member and he wrote some literatures on their practices. They are very conservative Muslims who believe in mysticism and *khalwa,* a doctrine of asceticism and commitment to prayer, reading and spiritual exercises. They believe in the intercession of their leader Abdl-al Quadir and they invoke his name in prayer.[26] They are not centralized in their organizational approach, but flexible in adapting their rituals to changing circumstances.[27]

Sheikh Ahmad Tijani (1737-1815) of Algeria founded Tijaniyya in 1781. It gained great popularity in North Africa and spread to West Africa in the 1830s. Al-Hajj Umar Tal Al-Futi is instrumental to the spread in West Africa. He made a visit to Sokoto and Borno in the1830's, and by 1937 the sect already had many followers in Northern Nigeria. Unlike other Islamic *tariqas*, they are not

---

"Boko Haram: Why We Struck in Kano," January 22, 2012. http://saharareporters.com/2012/01/22/boko-haram-why-we-struck-kano (accessed December 4, 2016). (Emphasis as in the original).

[26] Falola, *Violence in Nigeria*, 229.

[27] Abdul Raufu Mustapha and Mukhtar U. Bunza, "Contemporary Islamic Sects and Groups in Northern Nigeria," in *Sects and Social Disorder: Muslim Identities and Conflict in Northern Nigeria,* ed., Abdul Raufu Mustapha (Woodbridge: Boydell and Brewer Inc., 2014), 58.

opposed to trade or material acquisition insofar as such acquisition conforms to Islamic precepts. They do not insist on the seclusion of their women. They are promised salvation as long as they perform their taxing litanies and imitate the lifestyle of Mohammed.[28]

The relationship between the adherents of these two *tariqas* (orders or groups of Sufis) is hostile, as they compete vigorously for converts, territorial control and bragging rights of religious superiority.[29] Two Islamic scholars, Abdul Raufu Mustapha and Mukhtar Bunza, aptly capture the relationship between the two sects:

> Though the two Sufi orders share the introspection of Sufism, they differ in terms of their pantheons of saints, their social basis and their ritual. Importantly, they also competed for followership and influence in the prayer economy with the Qadiriyya accusing the Tijaniyya of emotional exuberance.[30]

There are Muslims who belong to neither of the two *tariqas*, and aggressively oppose Sufism; the Salafist sect is a case in point. For example, the Jama'atulzaltilBid'awa iqamat al-Sunna (Society for the Eradication of Innovation and the Reinstatement of Tradition) popularly known as Izala or JIBWIS, which emerged in the 1970's as an anti-Sufi movement. Formed under the leadership of their founder Shaikh Abubakar Gumi (1922-1992), this group adopted a seemingly religious-political ideology of the

---

[28] Falola, *Violence in Nigeria*. 230.

[29] Iwuchkwu, *Muslim-Christian Dialogue in Postcolonial Northern Nigeria*,127.

[30] Mustapha and Bunza, "Contemporary Islamic Sects and Groups in Northern Nigeria," 46.

Salafist Islamic group in opposition to the two already existing Sufi brotherhoods, whose religious ideologies emphasizes personal purification. In a contrary move, the Izala sets up its agenda of societal transformation, rejecting the ascription of a special role or reverence to the prophets. This led to mutual antagonism within the Muslim community.

Another popular Islamic sect in Nigeria is the Shia Muslim sect, which has its origin after the death of the prophet. The appointment of Abubakar as the first caliph by a gathering of some Islamic leaders around 632AD resulted in the fragmentation of Islam into two main sects. While the Shia believe that the right to the successor of the prophet as the leader of Islam is from God and as such falls to the family of the prophet, the Sunnis, believe in the replacement by appointment. This age-long dispute has been exacerbated over the years and has led to wars and differences in rituals and ideologies. The Shias have large populations in Iran, Syria, Iraq and a sizeable population in most parts of the world.[31] In contemporary Nigeria, the Shia sect has its followers among the members of Islamic Movement of Nigeria (IMN) or Muslim Brothers. This group originated in the 1970s amongst Islamic student group in some Northern Nigerian universities, who were frustrated by the corrupt political and social system in the country. They sought to restore the *shari'a* rule as the means to curb the socio-political situation of the country.[32]

---

[31] Christian W. Troll, "Catholicism and Islam," in *The Catholic Church and the World Religions: A Theological and Phenomenological Account,* ed., Gavin D'Costa (New York: T&K Clark International, 2011), 86-87.

[32] Ousmane Kane, *Muslim Modernity in Postcolonial Nigeria:*

Gradually, it metamorphized into an anti-state movement led by Shaikh El-Zakzaky, who held a very conservative Islamic ideology. El-Zakzaky advocates for a campaign of civil disobedience against the Nigerian state until Nigeria officially becomes an Islamic state. This group pledges allegiance to and receives support from the Iranian Shia sect. It believes and teaches the importance of martyrdom for the cause of Islam, gravitates towards a radical social revolutionary stance, and espouse confrontational ideologies.

In addition, several other Muslim sects exist in Nigeria including multiple split sub-sects within the major groups. In most cases, relations between these groups are fraught with disagreement, especially regarding the advocacy for or against punitive and strict practice of Islam, or aggression against the state and other religions. Some effects of these intra-religious conflicts among Muslims in Nigeria include radical reformation and occasionally, the emergence of extremist groups. The most recent and popular of these extremist sects is the terrorist group, Boko Haram, which pledges allegiance to Islamic State of Iraq and Syria (ISIS).

According to Umar Mamodu, the group emerged in 2002 as an aftermath of a clash between Sheikh Jafaar Adam and his disciple Mohammed Yusuf, at the MahammaduNdimi Mosque in Maiduguri-Borno State in northeastern Nigeria. The imbroglio began as a disagreement about Adam's moderate teachings and the more militant interpretation of the Qur'an by Yusuf, who is the originator of the Boko Haram sect. In 2002, Yusuf was

---

A Study of the Society for the Removal of Innovation and Reinstatement of Tradition (Leiden: Bill, 2003), 95.

expelled from the Ndimi Mosque Committee, later that year he built a mosque in the northeast of Nigeria to serve as a magnet for primary and secondary school pupils who, in response to his teachings, would abandon Westernized schools believing that Western education [*Boko*] is a sin [*Haram*]; hence the name Boko Haram.[33] Boko Haram opposes the westernization of Islam in Nigeria; it adopts a Salafist ideology that advocates for the return to the tradition of the forefathers of Islam. Their goal is to purify Islam in Nigeria and make the entire Nigeria an Islamic caliphate.[34] They attack both Christians and Muslims or anyone else who contravenes the dictates of their teachings. Religious instigated violence by the group has led to the premature death of thousands of people, with their reign of terror expanding across the borders of Nigeria to Chad, Cameroun, and Niger Republic.

This brief exploration of Muslims and Islam in Nigeria reveals the complexity and fragmentation within the religion in Nigeria. The implication of the divisiveness is that it impedes the actualization of interreligious dialogue with Christians, owing to the internal discordance, these Muslim groups cannot engage in efficient dialogue with one voice. Despite this unfortunate situation there have been areas of peaceful compromise, which will be explored later in this thesis.

---

[33]Umar Mamodu, "Boko Haram – the Beginning" *Boko Haram: How a Militant Islamist Group Emerged in Nigeria*, ed. Femi Owolade,http://www.gatestoneinstitute.org/4232/boko-haram-nigeria#_ftnref1(accessed November. 24, 2016).
[34] Virginia Comolli, *Boko Haram: Nigeria's Islamist Insurgency* (London: Hurt and Company, 2015), 19.

1.4. Christianity in Nigeria

The history of Christianity in Nigeria dates to the fifteenth and sixteenth centuries, when the first trade encounters between the Portuguese and some kingdoms in Southern Nigeria began. Some Portuguese Roman Catholic priests and some Augustinian monks established churches in Benin Kingdom, Itsekiri, and Warri. For two hundred years, the Catholic missionaries made regular trips to these areas in the company of the Portuguese traders. However, at the beginning of the eighteenth century, with the decline in the volume of commercial vessels making business trips to the region, missionary activities also declined. This earlier missionary expedition suffered several setbacks such as harsh weather, sickness among these missionaries due to malaria infections, and the use of proclamation-based evangelization that did not incorporate humanitarian services.

Missionary activity resumed around 1840, when the British established their trading base in Lagos and neighboring cities. After the abolition of the transatlantic slave trade, the freed slaves participated in evangelization, thereby furthering the propagation of Christianity. During this period, several Christian denominations made their entrance into Nigeria, including Anglicans, under the name, "Church Missionary Society" (CMS), the Wesleyan Methodist Church, the Presbyterian Church, the Baptist mission, and the Holy Ghost fathers, who established their mission in Onitsha in 1885. Missionary activities were taken into the hinterlands of Nigeria with the active participation of the indigenes.

Missionary activities in the late 1800s and early 1900s experienced a revolutionary twist that led to the establishment of independent churches. Owing to the attitudes of some of European missionaries toward their indigenous counterparts, some broke away from their mother churches but retained their names and rites.[35] From the mid-1900s, missionary activity in Nigeria burgeoned with the formation of indigenous churches. This was shortly followed by an upsurge of Pentecostal and Evangelical churches in the late 1900s. The evolution of Christianity in Nigeria is characterized by varying dispositions, attitudes and approaches of the diverse Christian denominations towards evangelization. The major Christian churches in Nigeria are classified into four groups, these include:

- Mainstream Christians, constituting Roman Catholics and Protestants.
- Evangelical Christian Churches including those having indigenous names but founded by European missionaries.
- Pentecostal independent churches founded by individuals or teams of charismatic preachers.
- Independent African Churches.

The mainstream Christians, including Roman Catholics and Protestants; Anglicans, Baptists, United, Lutherans, were mostly founded and sponsored by the West. Most of them have advanced and become financially self-reliant under the leadership of indigenous pastors, while some continue to rely on their foreign founders for support. They tend to remain under the umbrella of an international governing authority, like the papacy for the Roman

---

[35] Bénézet Bujo, *African Theology in its Social Context* (Maryknoll, NY: Orbis Books, 1992), 49.

Catholic Church, which resides in Rome. All the mainstream churches are more inclusive and tolerant in relating with other religions. Unlike the Evangelical and the Pentecostals, they do not usually engage in massive evangelization events, popularly referred to crusades (in Nigeria) for the purpose of converting those in other religions.

The Evangelical Christians are mostly groups that broke away from the mainstream Christian churches, by leaders who felt inspired to reform the existent mainstream spirituality and liturgy to one that is more relevant to the everyday life of the Africans. These Christian groups are led by indigenous pastors and often use indigenous languages in their worship. They believe that conversion is ultimately the action of the Holy Spirit. As such, they respect the peoples' choice of faith. They, however, tend to be religiously conservatives and very charismatic, though less radical than the Pentecostals. Some popular names in this category include the Evangelical Church of Christ in Nigeria (ECWA), Church of Christ in Nigeria (COCIN), Church of Christ in Nigeria (ECCN), and others with indigenous names like the HaddiyarEkklesiyarYan'uwa a Nigeria (HEKAN) and TarayyarEkklesiyyoyin Kristi A Nigeria (TEKAN).[36]

Pentecostal churches are autonomous churches that are mostly administered by their founders.[37] They tend to be

---

[36] Marinus Iwuchukwu, *Muslim-Christian Dialogue in Postcolonial Northen Nigeria: The challenges of Inclusive Cultural and Religious Pluralism* (New York: Palgrave Macmilliam, 2013), 122.

[37] SimonMary Asese Aihiokhai, Pentecostalism and Political Empowerment: The Nigerian Phenomenon," *Journal of Ecumenical Studies* 45, no.2 (Spring 2010), 250. (249-261)

fundamentalists and are very charismatic in their prayers and songs.[38] They lay emphasis on the baptism of the Holy Spirit and speaking in tongues. Pentecostals are characteristically less accommodating with those who do not hold their beliefs, including the members of the mainstream Christian churches and often arrogate the obligation of converting others to themselves. They are often vibrant and engage in massive evangelical outreach events. Furthermore, their messages are mostly financial prosperity, and break-throughs, which appeals to people in their situation. Hence, they are the largest growing population of Christians in Nigeria today. Describing the Pentecostals in Nigeria Akinade writes:

> Pentecostals do believe that there are genuine enemies, a group that includes one's opponent in

---

[38] The word 'fundamentalism' has assumed diverse meaning and interpretations in the contemporary era, in most cases connoting abuse and criticism. It is used for instance in social context by "liberals and Enlightenment rationalists against any group, religious or otherwise, that is critical about the absolutism of the post-Enlightenment ideologies. It is therefore important to note that in applying this word in this thesis, it refers to religious fundamentalism. In a broad sense, Malise Ruthven describes fundamentalism as "a religious way of being that manifest itself in a strategy by which beleaguered believers attempt to preserve their distinctive identities as individuals or groups in the face of modernity and secularization." This happens when individuals or traditionalist society is overtaken by globalization and plurality of religions, an aggressive effort to preserve their tradition results to fundamentalist tendencies. A crucial element traversing all fundamentalists is a literalist interpretation of the texts they revere. Such literal interpretation of religious texts tends to exclude those who do not belong to a particular religion. Cf. Malise Ruthven, *Fundamentalism: A Very Short Introduction*, (Oxford: Oxford University Press, 2007),4 – 9.

the faith and the devil in particular, whose main task is to hinder the spiritual growth and blessing of the Christian. The anointing of the Holy Spirit gives the power to overcome all the forces of darkness that contradict and contravene the qualities of an abundant life.[39]

Some of the Pentecostal Churches in Nigeria include Deeper Christian Life Ministry, Mountain of Fire and Miracles, Throne Room (Trust) Ministry, and Redeemed Christian Church of God (RCCG).

The last category of Christian groups in Nigeria is the African Independent Churches. These churches are African oriented.[40] Their leaders, though charismatic, are not flamboyant like other church leaders. They adopt more inclusive doctrine, and occasionally infuse elements of African Traditional Religion in their practice of Christianity. For instance, they uphold polygamy, which is socio-culturally acceptable in Africa.[41] Some of the popular African Independent Churches include the Aladura, Cherubim and Seraphim, Christa Church, and Brotherhood of Cross and Star. Interestingly, despite the ideological differences and dissimilarities in their approaches to evangelization, these Christian denominations co-exists peacefully.

Unfortunately, the relative peace among the Christian denominations aside, their relations with Muslim sects is characterized by confrontation and

---

[39] Akinade, *Christian Response to Islam in Nigeria*, 123.

[40] Deji Ayegboyin and S. Ademola Ishola, *African Indigenous Churches: An Historical Perspective* (Lagos, Nigeria: Greater Heights Publications, 1999), 24.

[41] Bujo, *African Theology in Its Social Context*, 48

conflicts, which sometimes lead to the needless destruction of human lives and material resources. In the section following, I will assess some of the causes of the conflicts between Christians and Muslims in Nigeria.

1.5. Contemporary Challenges to Christian-Muslim Co-existence in Nigeria

One of the primary obstacles hindering peaceful relations between Christians and Muslims is the rigid conservative approach to religion arising from doctrinal differences. Some conservative Christians lay claim to the uniqueness and universal salvific mediation of Jesus Christ. They base their arguments on the New Testament scripture, which affirms that Jesus Christ is the way, the truth and the life (Jn 14:6), the plenitude of revelation is uniquely given through Christ, because no one knows the Father except the Son and those to whom the Son wishes to reveal Him (Mt 11:27). Conservative Christians hold firm to the teaching that "there is no other name under heaven among men by which we must be saved" except the name of Christ (Acts 10:430).

In a similar vein, conservative Muslims hold firm to the teachings of the Qur'an, which sees Jesus as a prophet, "a messenger unto the children of Israel" to bring them a sign from there" (Qur'an 3:50). The Qur'an describes Jesus as "Messiah Jesus Son of Mary" both a prophet and a messenger (Qur'an 4:157); a "faultless slave" of Allah (Qur'an 19:19,30). The Qur'an, thus, denies the divinity of Jesus and the Mystery of the Trinity. It states that those who say, "Allah is the Messiah, Son of Mary," are unbelievers (Qur'an 5:17), even as are those who say, Allah is the third of three" (Qur'an 5:73). "O people of the scripture... say not Three'—Cease!" (Qur'an 4:171)[42] Rather, the Qur'an presents Muhammad as the "seal of the prophets" (*khatam al-anbiya*). He never claimed to be God but enjoined his followers to follow the only one God: "I am only a mortal like you. It is inspired in me that your God is One God, therefore take the straight path unto Him and seek forgiveness of Him" (Qur'an 41:6). Consequently, some conservative Muslims accuse the Jews and Christians of having falsified (*tahrif*) the scriptures. They claim that the Qur'an is the real authentic Word of God, for Allah himself dictated it, and Muhammed only transmitted it. It is thus regarded as the only miracle of the Qur'an.

In most cases, ultra-conservative elements within both religions in Nigeria have interpreted these doctrinal differences literally, and as a result, they resort into aggressive evangelization with the aim of converting others. In addition, they engage in contests for space and political position and these have led to suspicions and lack of trust, and in worst cases to violent clashes.

In the last twenty years, religious violence in Nigeria has claimed millions of human lives, and properties worth billions of dollars. Even though the primary goal of this book is not to chronicle the list of religious violence in Nigeria, I will provide instances of some of them, and their horrific and devastating effects, to provide a context for the necessity of highlighting theological responses that encourage peaceful relations while respecting religious commitment.

---

[42]Maurice Bormans, *Guidelines for Dialogue between Christians and Muslims* (New York: Paulist Press, 1990), 53-54.

One of the incidents of religious violence is the *Shari'a* riot of February 21-22, 2000 in Kaduna, which resulted in the loss of thousands of lives and displacement of peoples. The governor of the state at the time, Mohammed Ahmed Makarfi, had on February 3, 2000 introduced *Shari'a* law in a state with deep ethnic and religious divides, fuelling an already tensed situation.[43] Consequently, an outbreak of religious violence in which an estimated three thousand people lost their lives.[44] This event led to a reprisal attacks by Christians on Northerners, presumably, Muslims in Aba and Umuahia on February 28, 2000. The number of the dead is estimated at 450 people.

In February 18, 2006, a similar conflict occurred in Bornu State between Christians and Muslims. This time the violence was incited by the Danish cartoon publication of the image of the Prophet Mohammed in *Jyllands-Poten* newspaper. While such a publication was an unjustified provocation of the religious sensibilities of Muslims across the world, it does not justify the magnitude of violence it caused in Nigeria. Muslim youths went on a rampage; over 50 people were killed, and 30 churches destroyed; over 200 shops, 50 houses and 100 vehicles vandalized.[45]

---

[43] Olatunji E. Alao and Ayuba G. Mavalla, "Kaduna State Sharia Crisis of 2000: The Lessons and Challenges after Sixteen Years," *IOSR Journal of Humanities and Social Science* (IOSR-JHSS) 21, no.10 (October 2016),8-14.

[44] Isaac T. Sampson, "Religious Violence in Nigeria: Causal Diagnoses and Strategic Recommendation to the State Religious Communities" *African Centre for the Constructive Resolution of Disputes,* http://www.accord.org.za/ajcr-issues/%EF%BF%BCreligious-violence-in-nigeria/ (accessed February 6, 2017).

[45] Ibid.

Similarly, a bomb attack on Christians who were at a Catholic Church Christmas service, on December 25, 2011, left 45 people dead. Some died instantly, others from injuries sustained from the explosion. Over 80 others received treatment for various degrees of injuries.

Another instance of religious violence in Nigeria relates to Boko Haram's terrorist attacks. According to a recent report in *The Washington Post*, between 2011 and 2016, 17,402 people died, following 804 attacks.[46] In addition, more than 2.6 million Nigerians are presently internally displaced because of religious violence.[47] The horror unleashed by Boko Haram is not limited only to Christians, for the group has also targeted Muslims in recent times with bomb attacks on Mosques. The negative effects of religious violence in Nigeria cannot be underestimated; some of these include creating general insecurity, unemployment, food scarcity, crime and lack of development, all of which threaten the cohesion and existence of the nation state.

Other factors impeding interreligious dialogue in Nigeria is colonial intrusion and ethnocentrism. Ethnic affiliation positively gives people a sense of identity and personal membership in a society and constitutes a central part of African worldview. Regarding this interface between ethnicity, culture and religion in African worldview, Ogbonna Orji observes: "Ethnic groups sometimes use religion, not just as a means of self-

---

[46] Kevin Uhrmacher and Mary B. Sheridan, "The Brutal Tool of Boko Haram's Attacks on Civilians," *The Washington Post*, April 3, 2016. https://www.washingtonpost.com/graphics/world/nigeria-boko-haram/ (accessedMarch 9, 2017).
[47] Ibid.

determination, but to define themselves in opposition to other communities or groups. In this way religious identification is significant not only to the individual but also to the entire community."[48]Nigerians are divided across geopolitical, ethnic and religious lines. From its structural formation as a nation, Northern Nigeria is predominantly Muslim, while the South is predominantly Christian. The selfish political and economic structure created by the British colonialists widens this chasm further. When the British discovered that Islam had an organized leadership structure in the North that suited their indirect rule system of government and colonial enterprise, they prevented Christian missionaries from extending their activities to the North. The aim was to prevent Christians from rupturing their beneficial alliance with Fulani Muslim leaders, who collected taxes from the people for the British government.[49] Since then, the rift and deep divides between the Muslim North and the Christian South persisted in Nigeria.[50] Though in recent years the two religions have made progress towards peaceful co-existence in all parts of Nigeria, the presence of the Christians in the North or Muslims in the South (specifically the Southeast and Southsouth) continues to be perceived as an encroachment, and is frequently met with stiff resistance.

---

[48] Cyril Orji, "Ethnic and Religious Conflicts in Sub-Saharan Africa," *African Ecclesial Review*, *49,* no.1&2 (2007), 37-61.

[49] Frank A. Salamone, "Ethnic Identities and Religion," in *Religion and Society in Nigeria: Historical and Sociological Perspectives*, eds., J.K. Olupona and Toyin Falola (Ibadan, Nigeria: Spectrum Book Limited, 1991), 54.

[50] John Hatch, *Nigeria: A History* (London: Secker and Warburg, 1970), 13-15.

The tendency of Nigerians' to adhere tenaciously to their ethno-religious affiliations in their diverse socio-political and economic settings has negative implications for interreligious coexistence. For example, during elections, Southerners use the threat of possible Islamic domination and jihad to dissuade the electorates from supporting a Northerner or Muslim candidate and vice versa. In such instances, religion is politicized to the detriment of good governance and the peaceful co-existence of Nigerians. In the fight against corruption in Nigeria, most corrupt officials use their religious and political affiliations as immunity for evading the laws.[51] This explains why Nigeria loses billions of dollars every year to corrupt officials.

The deep-rooted mistrust and animosity between Christians and Muslims in Nigeria continuous to propel

---

[51]The greatest criticism of the leadership of the present Nigerian government of President Muhammad Buhari is the lopsidedness in his appointment of ministers and heads of military and parastatals who mostly come from the Muslim north. Equally, the fight against corruption seems also to have targeted those from other opposition parties. It is not uncommon to hear people describing his approach as the Islamization of Nigeria. See Daily Post, August 31, 2015, http://dailypost.ng/2015/08/31/buhari-is-president-for-the-north-fayose/ (accessed, December 7, 2017).

Joseph Kenny commenting on the challenges of politicization of religion in Nigeria, admonishes that "true equity can only be guaranteed if the government is neutral with regard to religion as such, not trying to judge the theological worth of any religion, but concerned only with the right of citizens to whatever conveniences are necessary for the practice of religion. See Joseph Kenny, "Christian-Muslim Relations in Nigeria,"*Christianity and Islam: The struggling Dialogue,* ed., Richard W. Rousseau (Montrose, Ridge & Row Press, 1985), 111-128.

countless acts of violence with the destruction of lives and properties and increased insecurity. Undeniably, the issue of interreligious dialogue in Nigeria needs to be tackled urgently. Therefore, to maintain peaceful co-existence between Muslims and Christians in Nigeria, the government and the citizens need to adhere to some prerequisite conditions.

1.6. The Prerequisites for Interreligious dialogue in Nigeria

In view of the numerous challenges impeding interreligious dialogue in Nigeria, this section discusses some of the prerequisites for effective interreligious dialogue and peaceful co-existence between Christians and Muslims in Nigeria.

1.6.1. Religious Freedom

For dialogue to strive there must be a conducive environment that permits the exercise of religious freedom, which is a fundamental human right. Interestingly, Christianity, Islam, and the Nigerian state all recognize the right to religious freedom. For instance, in *Dignitatis Humane,* the fathers of the Second Vatican Council affirmed the importance and necessity of religious freedom:

> [T]he human person has a right to religious freedom. Freedom of this kind means that everyone should be immune from coercion by individuals or of social groups and every human power, so that, within due limits, no men or women are forced to act against their convictions nor are any persons to be restrained from acting in accordance with their convictions

in religious matters in private or in public, alone or in association with others.[52]

While this conciliar teaching is aimed at protecting persons from violation, by either the state or religion, it is also a workable tool for meaningful dialogue from an interreligious perspective. Similarly, the Qur'an states: "Let there be no compulsion in religion" (Qur'an 2:256), while the Constitution of the Federal Republic of Nigeria upholds the principle of freedom of religion and association.[53] Over the years, the perceived threat to religious freedom has increased tensions between Christians and Muslims. For instance, when some of the Northern States declared *Shari'a* law as the law of their states, they did so without considering Christians living within the states who were inadvertently under compulsion to adhere to these laws. As expected, the Christians were apprehensive, and the issue generated heated national debates on its legality, and triggered some theological discussions from a religious angle. In reaction to the issue, the Archbishop of the

---

[52]Catholic Church, "Declaration on Religious Liberty,"in *The Basic Sixteen Documents: Vatican Council II Constitutions Decrees Declarations*, ed., Austin Flannery (Northport, New York: Costello Publishing Company, 1996), no. 1 (p.551).

[53] Article38. (1) of the 1999 Constitution of the Federal Republic of Nigeria states; "Every person shall be entitled to freedom of thought, conscience and religion, including freedom to change his religion or belief, and freedom (either alone or in community with others, and in public or in private) to manifest and propagate his religion or belief in worship, teaching, practice and observance." Cf. http://www.nigeria-law.org/ConstitutionOfTheFederalRepublicOfNigeria.htm. (accessed February 23, 2017).

Roman Catholic Archdiocese of Abuja, Cardinal John Onaiyekan writes:

> Aside from objecting to Shari'a on the ground that it enshrines a particular understanding of the will of God that may not be shared by Christians, Christians object to Shari'a as an imposition of the will of God by force of civil sanction. This amounts to a violation of people's right to freedom of conscience and God's will, as Christians understand it.[54]

Consequently, with the introduction of *Shari'a* in some Northern states, many Christians had to move from their base in the Northern States to cities in the South to retain their religious freedom. Eventually, this degenerated into violent conflicts and the destruction of properties. Such situations demonstrate how the need for religious freedom stands as a *sine qua non* for interreligious dialogue in the Nigerian context. The application of coercion in any form against religious freedom, distorts the much-needed safe space for dialogue, and makes dialogue practically unrealizable because it breeds insecurity and suspicion, which are inimical to socio-religious coherence.

---

[54] John Onaiyekan, "The sharia in Nigeria: A Christian View," *Bulletin on Islam and Christian-Muslim Relations in Africa* 5, no.3 (1987), 3-4. The Catholic Bishop's Conference of Nigeria (CBCN) also issued a communique on the development. Cf. Peter Schineller,*Pastoral Letters and Communiqués of the Catholic Bishops' Conference of Nigeria, 1960-2002: The Voice of the Voiceless* (Abuja, Nigeria: Gaudium Et Spes Institute, 2002), 146.

1.6.2. Openness

Dialogue will be fruitful if those engaging in it accede to mutual openness. They must first be open to the transforming grace of God through dialogue that enables one to appreciate God's works in the tradition of other religions.[55] Openness dispels ingrained bias and erroneous preconception about other religions. It could also inspire contriteness for the hurts of the past, forgiveness, and reconciliation, which is indispensable in the Nigerian context given her history of ethno-religious antagonism and socio-political violence.

Certainly, openness to learning the religious tenets of other religions is pertinent to overcoming religious bias. Interpersonal relationship between Christians and Muslims illuminates their shared humanity, thereby imbuing them with a different spiritual insight that cascades towards the same ultimate reality. As Catherine Cornille rightly points out: "In judging the truth of another religion solely on the basis of one's own religious framework and norms, dialogue also tends to become a monologue, and large missionary agenda."[56] This attitude aggravates suspicion and subsequently leads to breakdown of dialogue. YushauSodiq indicates that the suspicion of Christians harbored by Muslims of using dialogue to advance evangelization or conversion as one of the major obstacles to effectiveness of interreligious dialogue in Nigeria.[57]

---

[55] Cardinal Francis Arinze, *Meeting other Believers: The Risks and Rewards of Interreligious Dialogue* (Huntington, Indiana: Our Sunday Visitor Publishing Division, 1998), 95.

[56] Catherine Cornille, *The Im-possibility of Interreligious Dialogue* (New York: The Crossroad Publishing Company, 2008), 196.

However, the adoption of openness would prove valuable in eradicating interreligious fear and suspicion, and driving peaceful co-existence between Christians and Muslims in Nigeria.

1.6.3. Respect, Humility and Love

Not only are these three virtues crucial to the application of the idea of openness, they are inextricably connected and vital to the practice of dialogue. This is because it is impossible to respect someone you do not truly love, and to love truly one must be humble. Interreligious Dialogue is more enriching in a state of mutual respect and love. Our respect for the interlocutor in dialogue is an acknowledgement that the other person is an equal who has something to share in the discussion. In dialogue with people from other religion, it demands a humble attitude, a "less absolute attitude toward truth and a more open attitude toward the possible truth of another religious tradition."[58] Humility is important for effective dialogue, and ensuring respect of both the interlocutor and the concerned parties. Cornille asserts: "Openness and receptivity towards the truth of the other religion presupposes humble recognition of the constant limitation and therefore endless perfectibility of one's own religious understanding of the truth."[59] This implies that in engaging in dialogue between Christians and Muslims in Nigeria, it is important to take respect, humility and love, into thoughtful consideration, especially as these virtues are

---

[57] Sodiq, "Muslim Perception of Christians and Christianity in Nigeria," 149.

[58] Cornille, *The Im-possibility of Interreligious Dialogue*, 57

[59] Ibid., 10.

intrinsic to the teachings of both religions. The effect of this attitude is that dialogue becomes "an honest and sincere exchange between equals and based on a relationship of trust."[60]

Furthermore, Christianity and Islam preach the importance of love of neighbor, which originates from God's love for us. In the Bible, Jesus summarized the Decalogue as love of God and love of neighbor (Mark 12:29-31). He teaches that our love for God is concretized in our love for the least of our brethren (Mathew 25:31 - 46). While interpreting the implications of the love of God and neighbor, in his Encyclical Letter entitled, *Deus Caritas Est*, Pope Benedict XVI teaches that our brethren ideally encompasses every humanity, including those of other religions. According to Benedict XVI, this love "consists in the very fact that, in God and with God, I love even the person whom I do not like or even know."[61] In similar vein, Islam teaches undivided love and devotion to God (Qur'an 73:8). Prophet Muhammed explains: that none can claim to have faith except they love their brethren, as they love themselves, and love of neighbor is proven through concrete acts of charity (Quran 76:8-9).[62] Since the correlation of love of God and neighbor is a shared tenet of both religions, it provides a common ground for effective

---

[60]Darren J. Dias, "Fifty Years and the Learning: Development in the Roman Catholic Church's Encounter with Religions,"354.

[61]Pope Benedict XVI, Deus Caritas Est, http://w2.vatican.va/content/benedict-xvi/en/encyclicals/documents/hf_ben-xvi_enc_20051225_deus-caritas-est.html (accessed Dec. 6, 2017), no. 18.

[62] Cf. Sahih Muslim, Kitab al-Imam, 67-1, Hadith no.45, *A Common Word*; http://www.acommonword.com/the-acw-document/ (accessed December 7, 2017).

interreligious dialogue, and foundation for peaceful co-existence between Christians and Muslims in Nigeria.[63]

1.6.4. Commitment

It is crucial for followers of all religions to show commitment toward engaging constructively in dialogue with other religions. In this respect, commitment should assume twofold approach. First, it entails commitment to ones' religious convictions. What this implies is that, to be able to engage in effective dialogue with other religions, one must have a firm understanding of the doctrinal truth espoused by their religion. Such knowledge must be reinforced by the determination to apply it in dialogue for peaceful co-existence. Aloofness to the right teachings and complacency to the practice of the principles of one's religion hinders effective dialogue.[64]

Secondly, commitment should involve openness to dialogue with the religious other. Dialogue should not be regarded as the sole responsibilities of professionals who engage in theoretical dialogue. Rather, every ordinary believer regardless of their religion ought to engage with believers of other religions in the daily activities of their

---

[63] Ibid.

[64] Yusuff Jelili Amuda, observed that poor knowledge of the teachings of one's religion is one of the major obstacles to dialogue between Christians and Muslims in Nigeria. He advocates for what he calls religious literacy, citing that Islam provides, for its followers, the basis for tolerance and respect for other people. Yusuff Jelili Amuda, "Applying Sharia Principles of Religious Tolerance for the Protection of Children: Nigeria Religious Conflicts and Reconciliation among Muslims and Christians," in *Contemporary Muslim-Christian Encounters: Developments, Diversity and Dialogues, ed. Paul Hedges* (London: Bloomsbury, 2015), 83-97.

community. This spontaneous social dialogue is rewarding because it opens new avenues to the formation of deeper theological exchange and understanding of the religious doctrines and traditions of others.[65] The onus rests on religious leaders to inculcate this kind of mindset in their members by instructing them on the reach values of interreligious dialogue.[66]

1.7. Conclusion

In this chapter, efforts have been made to stage the context in which the interreligious dialogue in Nigeria is taking place and may more fully develop. A brief history of Nigeria, the emergence of Islam and Christianity and the major challenges militating against interreligious dialogue in Nigeria reveal the task this work aims to tackle. However, a brief look at the prerequisites for interreligious dialogue, which seems almost absent in Nigeria, also reveals the challenges of engaging in effective dialogue in the Nigerian context. Such challenges lead me to the next chapter, which will explore various paradigms in Christian theology of religion and analyze them with the aim of projecting the paradigm that promotes the qualities that enhance effective dialogue.

---

[65] Social Dialogue, which consists of Dialogue of Life and Action is discussed in detail in the fourth chapter.

[66] There are other contemporary factors militating against effective dialogue in Nigeria such as: Inept Governance, Corruption, Poverty and others. These are presumed in my discussions above, as they are related to the factors already listed. For further reading see, Thaddeus Byimui Umaru. *Christian-Muslim Dialogue in Northern Nigeria: A Socio-Political and Theological Consideration* (p. 72). Xlibris. Kindle Edition.

Chapter Two

Making the Case for Theological Inclusivism

2.1. Introduction

The post-modern society has witnessed an unprecedented advancement in communication technology and transportation, which have shrunken the gap existing between peoples, cultures and religions. In addition, the mass migration of people displaced by wars or economic and socio-political upheavals has led to the increasingly intermingling of people from diverse religious and cultural backgrounds. Regarding this trend, Allan Race observes that "days of religious and cultural isolation is over [...] changing patterns of mobility have shattered older conceptions of the religious history of the world, which viewed these faiths as confined, culturally and geographically, within particular boundaries."[67] While this fact is incontrovertible, there remains the question of how people respond to the reality of a pluralistic cultural and religious world.

The doctrines of peoples' religion reflect in their reaction to the people of other religions and how the interpretations of other religions are represented through the prism of categories and major creeds of their own faith. Therefore, while some people are more open to other religions as companions making the same journey, albeit through different routes to the same ultimate goal, others see the religious other as incompatible to their religious beliefs and aspiration, and as such, in need of conversion to the true religion. Others remain in-between these two extremes. Thus, while laying claim to superiority of creed,

---

[67] Race, *Christians and Religious Pluralism*, 1.

they may still acknowledge that other religions equally embody the truth of religion for its members. From a Christian theological perspective, a myriad of studies analyzing the possible responses of Christians to religious pluralism exists, especially in the area known as the "Christian theology of religions." The renowned Catholic theologian, Jacques Dupuis (1923-2004) describes Christian theology of religions as "the study of the various traditions in the context of the history of salvation and in their relationship to the mystery of Jesus Christ and the Christian Church."[68]

The issue of the possibility of salvation outside the Christian faith and the way each Christian tradition perceives it largely determines their disposition towards dialogue with other faiths. To this effect, scholars of the theology of religions have tried to classify the emerging paradigms in the theology of religions. A good example is the Christian theologian, Owen C. Thomas, whose book entitled, *Attitudes Towards Other Religions*(1969), has been described as a watershed in the classification of Christians' response to other faiths, namely: rationalism, romanticism, relativism, exclusivism, dialectic, reconception, tolerance, dialogue, Catholicism, and presence.[69] However, in spite of being applauded as a landmark achievement, Thomas' work has been criticized for being "a conglomeration of logical positions, emotive states, and simple demographics."[70] Other theological

---

[68] Jacques Dupuis, *Towards a Christian Theology of Religious Pluralism* (Maryknoll: Orbis Books,1997), 8.

[69] Owen C. Thomas, *Attitudes Towards Other Religions* (London: SCM Press, 1969), 245-260.

[70] Terry Muck, "Instrumentality, Complexity, and Reason: A

works such as Carl F. Hallencreutz's, *New Approaches to Men of Other Faiths,*[71] and Eric J. Sharpe's, *Faith Meets Faith*, are further contributions towards the tracking of different trends in the Christian attitude to religious plurality.[72] These writings are primarily concerned with the "historical and theoretical patterns, mainly in the present century, of the changing nature of the Christian theorizing about the other faith."[73]

The work of Alan Race, *Christianity and Religious Pluralism,* which offers a threefold paradigm namely exclusivism, inclusivism and pluralism has dominated Christian Theology of Religions. Summarily, the arguments embodied in these three paradigms can be described respectively as follow: first, to claim that non-Christians do not have access to salvation; second, to develop a theological principle that explains how non-Christians can be granted Christian salvation; and third, to argue that all religions have equal access to a universal form of salvation.[74] According to J. Andrew Kirk, Race's tripartite paradigm captures the customary way most authors, in recent years discuss the relationship between Christianity and non-Christian religions.[75] Nevertheless, Kirk dismisses Race's

---

Christian Approach to Religions,"*Buddhist-Christian Studies* 22 (2002), 115 - 121.

[71] Carl F. Hallencreutz, *New Approaches to Men of Other Faiths* (WCC, Geneva 1970), 1-5

[72] Eric J. Sharpe, *Faith Meets Faith* (SCM Press, London 1977), 1-4

[73] Race, *Christians and Religious Pluralism*, 7.

[74] Mara Brecht, "What's the use of Exclusivism" *Theological Studies*73, no.1 (2012), 33-54.

[75] J. Andrew Kirk, *What is Mission? Theological Exploration* (Minneapolis: Fortress Press, 2000),127.

paradigm as less satisfactory because each division includes elements of the others. He argues that exclusivism "gives an immediate impression of narrow-mindedness, even bigotry; pluralism conjures up the image of relativism, even a lack of concern; inclusivism, however, appears to emphasis open-mindedness and tolerance."[76] Kirk's disavowal of Race's model leads to his propounding of the concepts of particularity, generality and universality as a replacement of Race's threefold paradigm respectively. A theological review of Kirk's model reveals a repetition of the core ideas of Race's paradigm, as such, it lacks theoretical novelty.

Gavin D'Costa, who was a proponent of this paradigm, later changed his mind and vigorously discredits its adequacy in categorizing the different responses to the plurality of religions. For instance, D'Costa argues that Race's depiction of pluralism is actually a covert form of exclusivism, since it does not affirm all traditions as tradition specific, but instead grounds Christian pluralism on western liberal modernity.[77]

In his work, *Introducing Theologies of Religions*, Paul Knitter attempts to formulate a new paradigm that would accommodate those whose theological positions to the reality of religious pluralism seem not to have been well represented in Race's tripod paradigm. Knitter's four models' classification include replacement, fulfilment, mutuality and acceptance. Knitter's analysis of replacement model corresponds to Race's exclusivism paradigm, his fulfilment model corresponds with Race's inclusivism

---

[76] Ibid, 127-128.

[77] Gavin D'Costa, *The Meeting of the Religions and the Trinity* (Edinburgh: T & T Clark, 2000), 22, 37.

paradigm, and his mutuality model resembles Race's pluralism paradigm, while acceptance model is the added model that differentiates his model from Race's typologies. Acceptance model holds the view that "religious traditions of the world are different, and we have to accept those differences."[78] Also, acceptance model does not hold up "superiority of any religion," nor search for "common ground" but "accepts the diversity of all faith."[79]

Over the years, other models in theology of religions have emerged. Worthy of note here is Peter Shineller' spectrum. It consists of four paradigms for considering Christians understanding of the religious these include: first, ecclesiocentric universe, exclusive Christology; second, Christocentric universe, inclusive Christology; third, theocentric universe, normative Christology; fourth, theocentric universe, non-normative Christology. The first is characterized by an exclusive and explicit faith in Christ, with the Church being the sole means of salvation. The second allows for anonymous or implicit Christian faith as way to salvation. It maintains that there is only one economy of salvation. "Jesus is the normative revelation of God and is constitutive of the work of God in the world. He is the mediator of all other revelations, and the salvation which can be attained in the world first occurs in Jesus and occurs elsewhere through him."[80] The third position is theocentric and maintains that God's love has been operative everywhere and always but expressed most

---

[78]Paul F. Knitter, *Introducing Theologies of Religions* (Maryknoll, NY: Orbis Books, 2002), 173.

[79] Ibid.

[80] Peter J. Schineller, "Christ and Church: A Spectrum of Views," *Theological Studies* 37 no. 4 (1976), 552.

clearly in the person and work of Jesus. It implies that Jesus Christ is neither the exclusive savior nor the constitutive savior, but the normative savior. The fourth proposes that there are many mediators of salvation, and Jesus Christ is only one of them.[81] The subtlety of Shineller's typology evinces that the second and third spectrums could be located in Race's inclusivism, although versions of the third could be included in the fourth, which resonates with Race's pluralism. Therefore, in contrast to the complexity of Shineller's typology, Race's less complex model could be more easily adopted in Nigerian context and incorporated into related theological assessments.

Regardless of the criticisms mentioned above, this work appropriates Race's threefold paradigm. This is because, I believe that given the multiplicity and ever-evolving nature of Christian's responses to the plurality of religions, theological theorizing of spectrums and models can never exhaustively accommodate every individual response, especially as the grouping overlap each other. Race's paradigm is relevant here because it is a "broad typological framework within which most of the current Christian theologies of religions can be placed."[82] It is also the most prominent and accepted model among theologians of Christian theology of religions. Paul Hedges endorses Race's paradigm and describes it as "descriptive and heuristic."[83] It is functional, less complex, and aptly suited for addressing the trends in a Nigerian context.

---

[81] Ibid., 555 – 562.

[82] Race, *Christians and Religious Pluralism*, 7.

[83] Paul Hedges, "Reflection on Typologies: Negotiating a Fast-Moving Discussion," *Christian Approaches to Other Faiths*, eds. Alan Race and Paul Hedges (London: SCM, 2008), 22.

In the section that follows, I will critically examine religious responses to pluralism within the Nigerian context through the lenses of Race's paradigm. My analysis postulates inclusivism as the most appropriate paradigm for effective interreligious dialogue in Nigeria. Because the subject of interreligious dialogue is broad and has substantial theological works, an exhaustive analysis of all the scholars and the criticism of their varied positions are impossible within the scope of this book. Bearing this limitation in mind, I will briefly present the three paradigms, making the case for inclusivism as a feasible Christian position in approaching dialogue with other religions, especially with Islam as the interlocutor in the dialogue.

2.2. Exclusivism

Exclusivism holds that salvation is only possible through an explicit faith in Jesus Christ. According to Race, the implication of this belief is that Christianity "counts the revelation in Jesus Christ as the sole criterion by which all religions including Christianity, can be understood and evaluated."[84] This position is typically generated by faith commitment.[85] It is *a priori*, top-down and Christocentric. It is ultimately based on an interpretative response to other religions on New Testament's scriptural passages. Some examples of these passages include: "There is salvation in no one else, for there is no other name under heaven given among mortals

---

[84]Race,*Christians and Religious Pluralism*, 11.

[85] John Hick, "The Possibility of Religious Pluralism: A Response to Gavin D'Costa," in *Religious Studies* 33, no.2 (1997), 166-166.

by which we must be saved" (Acts 4:12); "For no one can lay any foundation other than the one that has been laid; that foundation is Jesus Christ" (1Cor3:11); "There is one mediator between God and humankind; Christ Jesus" (1 Tim. 2:5); "I am the way the truth and the life. No one comes to the Father except through me" (John 14:6); "Whoever has the Son has life; whoever does not have the Son of God does not have life" (1 John 5:12). "Whoever believes in the Son has eternal life; whoever disobeys the Son will not see life but must endure the wrath of God" (John 3:36). These scriptural passages are sacred for the proponents of exclusivism and to be observed and believed as expressed. Kirk describes this position as 'particularity' when he writes:

> Particularity is the belief that God's gift of salvation is available only through the atoning death of the historical person, Jesus of Nazareth, and is appropriated through explicit faith in Jesus and ratified by baptism and membership of Christian community… that God has provided only one way of salvation and that there must be a conscious response to the offer.[86]

Prior to the Second Vatican Council, the relationship between the Roman Catholic Church and other religions was characterized by exclusivism. This exclusivist position was evident in the Roman Catholic Church's denial of salvation to those outside its fold, and vividly expressed in the infamous dictum: *"Extra Ecclesia Nulla Salus"* (outside the Church there is no salvation). Wayne Teasdale aptly

---

[86] Kirk, *What is Mission?* 128.

captures the meaning and implications of this exclusivist position:

> Salvation, or eternal beatitude with God, with the Trinity, angels, and saints, is only possible in and through the mediation of the Catholic Church and those in union or communion with the Church. This possibility of salvation is achieved through the salvific act of Jesus Christ through the redemption that occurred in the Incarnation when he became a human being while remaining fully divine.[87]

The history of this teaching is based specifically on 1 Peter 3:18-21, where the image of Noah's Ark was used as the image of the Church. Just as eight persons survived the flood, saved in Noah's Ark, likewise, those who are baptized into the Church are saved through water and the Holy Spirit in the name of Jesus Christ. In the second century, Ignatius of Antioch associated the Ark with the Church, but not with salvation. The Greek father, Origen, emphasized the necessity of the church for salvation, he declares: "Let no one fool himself; outside this house, i.e. outside the Church no one is saved; for, if someone goes outside, he becomes responsible for his own death."[88] Similarly, in the third century, Clement of Alexandria relates salvation to membership with the Church.

Although Cyprian of Carthage projected exclusivism in his teaching, it gained popularity and tractionin the fourth and fifth century through the teaching of Augustine of

---

[87] Wayne Teasdale, *Catholicism in Dialogue: Conversation Across Traditions* (New York: A Sheed and Ward Book, 2004), 82.

[88] Ibid., 84.

Hippo who believes that the church is a "concrete and universal community, willed by Jesus himself, which one has to accept with humility as the proper environment of faith and the way to salvation."[89] The official documents of the church at the time emphasizes the notion of the church's indispensability for salvation. For example, Pope Boniface VIII on November 18, 1302 issued a bull: *UnamSanctam*, which declares: "We firmly believe and absolutely confess this (Church) outside of which there is neither salvation nor forgiveness." The bull argued that at the time of the flood, there was one ark of Noah, which represents the Church, and all living creature outside of the ark faced destruction. This teaching also gave impetus to the declaration of the Council of Florence (1442) in the bull, *Cantante Domino,* which extended no salvation even to the Jews:

> The holy Roman Catholic Church [...] firmly believes, professes and preaches that "no one remaining outside the Catholic Church, not only pagans, but Jews or heretics and schismatics, can become partakers of eternal life; but they will go to the eternal fire prepared for the devil and his angels.[90]

---

[89] Tarsicius J. Van Bavel, "Church," in *Augustine through the Ages: An Encyclopedia*, ed. Allan D. Fitzgerald O.S.A (Grand Rapids: Eerdmans, 1999), 6.

[90] Cf. Josef Neuner and Jacque Dupuis, eds., *The Christian Faith in the Doctrinal Documents of the Catholic Church* (Westminster, MD: Christian Classics, 1975), 309-310

This assertion summates the exclusivist attitude of the Roman Catholic Church to other religions before the convocation of the Second Vatican Council.

Among the conservative Protestant Churches, the Evangelicals and Pentecostal churches, there exist also an exclusivist approach to relationship with other religions. I will employ the teachings of the famous Swiss Reformed theologian, Karl Barth (1886-1968) as an example of the theological position of these Christian groups. For Barth, the knowledge of the truth or the knowledge of God is only revealed by God and made known to us by his grace. Therefore, any attempt by religion to project knowledge of God is unbelief. According to Barth:

> Revelation is God's self-offering and self-manifestation. Revelation encounters man on the presupposition of the fact that man's attempts to know God from his own standpoint are wholly and entirely futile; not because of any necessity in principle, but because of a practical necessity of fact. In revelation God tells man he is God, and that as such he is his Lord.[91]

The main idea here is the belief in God's self-revelation and not by the act of religion. Barth further argues that God's self-revelation in Christ is the definite manifestation of God's self to redeem us, because:

> The revelation of God in Jesus Christ maintains that our justification and sanctification, our

---

[91] John Hick, and Brian Hebblethwaite, *Christianity and Other Religions: Selected Readings* (Oxford: Oneworld, 2001), 8.

conversion and salvation, have been brought about and achieved once and for all in Jesus Christ. And our faith in Jesus Christ consists in our recognizing and admitting and affirming and accepting the fact that everything has actually be done for us once and for all in Jesus Christ.[92]

Barth surmises that since no religion can achieve revelation by itself, revelation can adopt religion and mark it off as a true religion.[93] Thus, there is true religion just as there is a justified sinner, since true religion and justification is an act of grace made possible by the revelation of God in Christ, and that religion is Christianity. Precisely, Barth sees other religions as human fabrications and denies the possibility of both revelation and salvation to non-Christian religions. Paul Knitter describes this form of exclusivism as "Total Replacement." Knitter explains:

> They feel that it really allows for no value, no presence of God, in other religions, viewing them as entirely man-made, as obstacles to, rather than conduits for, God's love. In theological terms, there is neither revelation nor salvation in the world of other religions. And that means the only kind of dialogue Christians can have with persons of other faith is one in which Christianity tries to get to know those

---

[92] Karl Barth, "The Revelation of God as the Abolition of Religion," in *Christianity and other Religions: Selected Readings,* eds., John Hick and Brian Hebblethwaite (Oxford: One World Publication, 2001), 11.

[93] Ibid.

faith better in order to replace them with Christianity.[94]

There are other theologians who despite having an exclusivist approach to religion, made case for "general revelation" or God's presence in other religions. While they do not ascribe salvation in and through these religions, they affirm to the authenticity of divine revelation in the religions of the world. This position is backed by scriptural passages such as Rom. 1:20; 2:15, which states:

> Ever since the creation of the world God's eternal power and divine nature, invisible though they are, have been understood and seen through the things God has made... What the law requires is written on their hearts, to which their own conscience also bears witness.

What Paul is implying here is that God reveals himself to people through their consciences and through nature. Another New Testament passages in support of this view states: "In past generations, God allowed all the nations to follow their own ways; yet God has not left you without a witness in doing good – giving you rain from heaven and fruitful seasons, and filling you with food and your heart with joy" (Acts 14:16).This passage indicates God's presence through nature, this is reiterated in the gospel of John 1:1-14, which confirms the presence of the Word from the beginning, and that the Word is the light which shines in the darkness.

---

[94] Knitter, *Introducing Theologies of Religions,* 33.

The above-mentioned passages indicate God's revelation and presence throughout the world, among peoples and religions. Hendrick Kraemer (1888-1965), while identifying with Barth on the *sui generis* character of revelation in Jesus Christ, nevertheless, questions Barth's failure to explain how God works outside of the sphere of revelation, and why he rejects a "point contact" between God's revelation and human consciousness.[95] In the same vein, the prominent Swiss Protestant (Reformed) theologian, Emil Brunner (1889-1966) argues that human beings, who are made in the image of God, have the capacity to receive the revelation or Word of God and the capacity to reject it despite his sinful state. Simply put, humans are not just passive recipients of revelation, but participate in limited ways in apprehending God's revelation.[96] Interpreting Brunner, Alister McGrath points out that:

> However, revelation is to be understood, it involves human cognition and perception, which recognize it for what it actually is. Revelation takes place within history, culture, and the natural order, and does not bypass its categories [...] Revelation may involve the interpretation of historical events, the hearing of the word of God, the reading of Scripture, experience of the presence of God, or reflection on the natural world... Yet that process of interpretation and

---

[95] Hendrick Kraemer, *The Christian Message in a Non-Christian World* (Grand Rapids, MI: Kregel Publication, 1956), 133.

[96] Emil Brunner, "Nature and Grace," in *Natural Theology*, eds., Emil Brunner and Karl Barth, trans. Peter Fraenkel (London, UK: Geoffrey Bles, 1946), 15–64.

appropriation also includes human perception, which simply cannot be eliminated for the sake of theological convenience.[97]

Despite their divergent views on the nature of revelation, the proponents of exclusivism have a common consensus on Jesus Christ as the sole mediator of salvation. This stance, however, has provoked lots of criticisms regarding its viability in interreligious dialogue. I would briefly highlight some of these criticisms.

The claim to true revelation in Jesus Christ as the only path to salvation by Christian exclusivists inadvertently accuses other religions of falsehood. According to LesslieNewbigin: "The message of Jesus Christ, of the unique incarnate Lord crucified by the powers of the Law, morals and piety and raised to the throne of cosmic authority, confronts the claim of every religion with radical negation."[98] The question arises: will all the adherents of other religions end up in hell because they do not explicitly profess their faith in Jesus Christ? Wilfred Cantwell Smith provides a rational response, contending that such stance is not Christian, because it implies having a "faith that can be undermined by God's saving one's neighbour."[99] The problem with relentless exclusivism is its inability to

---

[97]Alister E.McGrath, *The Open Secret: A New Vision for Natural Theology*(Malden, MA: Blackwell, 2008), 107-108

[98] Lesslie Newbigin, *The Open Secret: Sketches for a Missionary Theology* (Grand Rapids: Eerdmans, 1978), 177.

[99] Wilfred Cantwell Smith, "The Christian in a Religiously Plural World," *Christianity and Other Religions: Selected Readings,* 45.

reconcile "a truly Christian charity and perceptivity with doctrinal adequacy."[100]

While these responses do not address the epistemological questions raised by the theology of exclusivism such as the uniqueness of Christ's revelation, they highlight its apparently contradictoriness to the Christian's teachings on the love of neighbour. Regarding the claim of absolute truth and unique revelation in Jesus Christ, the exclusivist relies solely on New Testament, however, there are also passages in the Bible that are antithetical to those. In addition, historical critical enquiries into the scriptures have revealed some socio-cultural influence on the interpretation of the Bible. Additionally, other religions could make such claims to absolute truth with reference to their own scriptures, since faith goes with *a priori* theoretical proposition and assumptions. What of those whose socio-cultural conditions made it practically impossible for them to embrace the Christian religion, though they lived a life of love, but could not explicitly profess Christian faith? Does it mean there will be no salvation for them? While the Christian exclusivist position might be applicable within a Christian context, it will not be proactive in interreligious dialogue.

The unresolved questions of the exclusivist position regarding the salvation of non-Christians, and the troubles it has created in the world, especially as some fundamentalist elements have latched on to them as reasons to reject, fight and even kill people of other religious persuasion, has led to oppositional theological responses to exclusivism in Christian theology of religions.

---

[100] Ibid.

2.3. Pluralism

Pluralism considers every religion as a valid path to salvation or liberation of their members, and Jesus Christ is considered as only one path among many paths that exist. According to D'Costa:

> By "pluralist" I mean a range of features, shared by writers who use this term of self-description, to indicate the broad assumption that: all religions (with qualifications) lead to the same divine reality; there is no privileged self-manifestation of the divine; and finally, religious harmony follow if tradition-specific (exclusivist) approaches which allegedly claim monopoly over truth are abandoned in favour of pluralist approaches which recognize that all religions display the truth in different ways.[101]

Unlike the Christocentric and Ecclesiocentric stance adopted by exclusivists, pluralists are theocentric or God-centred and Reality-centered. They base their arguments on the impossibility of any one religion to claim full knowledge of the mysteries of the infinite God within the limits of our finite human capacity, because "all human knowledge is historically conditioned or socially constructed and therefore limited."[102] As Smith aptly affirms: "the finite cannot comprehend the infinite."[103] For this reason, pluralists reject any absolute claim of the truth of religion, rather

---

[101] Gavin D'Costa, *The Meeting of Religions and the Trinity* (Edinburgh: T&T Clark, 2000), 19.

[102] Knitter, *Introducing Theologies of Religion,* 125.

[103] Ibid.

they contend that "religions must acknowledge their need of each other if the full truth about God is to be available to mankind."[104] In the discussion that follow, I will briefly examine the works of two theologians, John Hick (1922-2012) and Paul Knitter, who advocate pluralism as an effective approach toward interreligious relationships.

Hick argues for a revolution or paradigm shift in the Christian approach to other religions. He likens the suggested revolution to the Copernican revolution, and it implies transforming the notion of Jesus as the centre of revelation and salvation to God as the centre. According to Hick:

> [It] involves a… radical transformation in our conception of the universe of faiths and the place of our own religion within it…. a paradigm shift from a Christianity-centered to a God-centered model of the universe of faiths. One then sees the great world religions as different human responses to the one divine reality, embodying different perceptions, which have been formed in different historical and cultural circumstances.[105]

The aim of this theory is to de-privilege any religion of superiority claims and imperialist approach in relations to other religions.

Hick's concept of salvation among religions is the transformation of the individual person from self-

---

[104] Race, *Christians and Religious Pluralism*, 72.

[105] John Hick, *God and the Universe of Faiths* (New York: St. Martin's Press, 1973), 131.

centredness to a reality-centeredness, which people can find through their various religious affiliations. He does not simply affirm every tradition in an utter relativism, but rather insists that "religious traditions and their various components…have greater or less value according as they promote or hinder the salvific transformation."[106] Thus, in principle religious phenomena can be assessed, and the basic criterion is the extent to which they promote or hinder the great religious aim of salvation or liberation.

Hick discovers a common value among major religions. This value is perceptible among individuals who are considered as models or saints in their religions. They are people who have transcended ego point of view and are centred in the manifestation of the Real, towards other human being in love and compassion.[107] This commonality, could prompt a philosopher to conclude that this ethical fruit has one common root. Therefore, Hick argues for pluralism based on moral equivalence. Hick states: "We find that both the virtues and the vices are, so far as we can tell, more or less equally spread among the population, of whatever major faith – and here I include Humanism and Marxism as major (though secular rather than religious) faiths."[108] Hick surmises that no one religious tradition can be singled out as manifestly superior, and there is no agreed definition of sainthood, but claims that he has no difficulty in recognizing its absence.[109]

---

[106] John Hick, *An Interpretation of Religion* (Basingstoke: MacMillan, 1989), 300.

[107] Ibid., 301.

[108] John Hick, *A Christian Theology of Religions* (Louisville: Westminster John KnoxPress, 1995), 13.

[109] John Hick, "The Non-Absoluteness of Christianity," in *The*

This proposition has attracted some criticisms, among which is that Hick's ontological foundation for making the moral judgement of who qualifies as a saint is questioned. Because, his position is based on the worldview of the Western liberal ideology of the twentieth century evident in his adoption of Kantian theory. The implication of this ideological stance is that Hick is inadvertently imposing his religious ideology on other religions, since every religion is a product of a particular culture and is a mere appearance of the Real. Furthermore, there is an apparent alterity and ambiguity in the interpretation of religion's understanding of the aim of life and path of life. Reflecting on this issue, Pannenberg notes that if the use of the term salvation refers to actual transformation of human life from self-centered to reality-centered, it is inarguably obtainable in every religion, but this does not depict Christian concept of salvation. Pannenberg argues:

The idea need not be restricted to judicial act in the sense described by Hick as alternative to his own view, but it belongs to the dimension of eschatological belief rather than to present experience. As such it is bound up with the truth of Jesus' claim to eschatological finality (see Lk 12:8 and parallels).[110]

Myth of Christian Uniqueness: Toward a Pluralistic Theology of Religion, eds., John Hick and Paul Knitter(Maryknoll, NY: Orbis books, 1988), 30.

[110] Wolfhart Pannenberg, "Religious Pluralism and Conflicting Truth Claims: The Problem of a theology of the World Religions," in *Christian Uniqueness Reconsidered: The Myth of a Pluralistic Theology of Religions*, ed., Gavin D'Costa (Maryknoll, NY: Orbis Books, 1990), 96-106.

This has implications on truth claims by religions. Hick has been disparaged by critics for playing down the question of truth claim in his proposition on theology of religions, especially when it is obvious that different religions make truth claims that are mutually irreconcilable. For example, the Christianity claim that Jesus is God and through him God grants salvation to all peoples is different from Islamic understanding of the person of Jesus nor do they believe Jesus has any direct role in human salvation.

There is a profound link between truth claim to the 'aim of life' and the 'path of life' especially in Christian religion. For example, the acceptance of the truth claims on incarnation among Christians cannot be separated from the eschatological hope, which forms the ontological bases for their embrace of the teachings and life of Jesus as a necessary path for salvation. It is in view of this that LesslieNewbigin cautions:

> It would seem that the proposal to sever the search for salvation from the business of distinguishing truth from error, is a sign of the approaching death of a culture. What is certain is that this kind of pluralism will simply crumble in the presence of a confidence and vigorous claim to know the truth – such a claim as Islam is at present making with increasing vigor in the contemporary world.[111]

---

[111] Lesslie Newbigin, "Religion for the Marketplace," in *Christian Uniqueness Reconsidered: The Myth of a Pluralistic Theology of Religions*, ed., Gavin D'Costa (Maryknoll, NY: Orbis Books, 1990), 135-148.

To downplay the issue of truth-claim or sever it from the search of salvation, liberation or enlightenment for the sake of harmony is tantamount to what D'Costa regards as spurious harmony, because it takes no one seriously by discounting a religion's absolute claim. In which case, interreligious dialogue will become an exercise in frivolity and vanity.[112]

To account for the transcendental basis of all religions while affirming their diverse and incompatible assertions about the Real itself (*ansich*) and its manifestations, Hick employs Immanuel Kant's epistemological theory on the distinction between phenomena and noumena. While the noumenal exists independently and outside of human perception, the phenomenal world is the world as it appears to our human conscientiousness. Applying this to the religions, Hick argues that we cannot have immediate perception of "the Real itself" or God, because religious experience of God is mediated by the finite categories of religion, including its historical, social and psychological make up. In this way, the different religions of the world "constitute different ways of experiencing, conceiving, and living in relation to an ultimate divine Reality which transcends all our varied versions of it."[113] The implication is that whatever the religions present as the Real is only presented in myths, symbol and metaphors, since the Real transcends immediate access and comprehension. Hence,

---

[112] Gavin D'Costa, "Pluralist Arguments: Prominent Tendencies and Methods," in *Catholic Engagement with World Religions: A Comprehensive Study*, eds., Karl Joself Becker, Ilaria Morali (Maryknoll, New York: Orbis Books, 2010), 336.

[113] John Hick, *An Interpretation of Religion* (Basingstoke: MacMillan, 1989), 14.

there is only one religious *noumenon* with multiple religious *phenomena*. This suggests that the apparent differences between religions exist because of inadequate or non-exhaustive interpretation of the ultimate Real. Similarly, the different religions exist because of finite human interpretations, all of which indirectly express a common referent that exceeds their grasp. For example, doctrines are like linguistic fingers pointing at the moon (to use a Zen parable), the 'real' referent being beyond themselves and only implied. So, unity lies beyond religious comprehension.[114]

Hick's theological proposition on religions' impossible immediate knowledge of the Real, also raises the question of how himself can account for such knowledge. Since you can only make such claims, if you yourself have the superior knowledge of the spiritual reality. Nevertheless, if Hick's proposition is followed, it implies that he is speaking from a particular perspective that is influenced by his own tradition or historical background, since no one can gain immediate access to the Real. As such, Hick's claims to independent access to the true reality of God, is akin to what Knitter calls "creeping imperialism;" the imposition of one's own particular view point on all others in the name of universality.[115] In addition, Mark Heim opposes the idea of a common ground as projected by Hick, and argues that those who project God as the center or common ground for all religions without identifying which God they are referring, makes themselves God.[116]

---

[114] Ng Kam Wing, "Pluralism and Particularity of Salvation in Christ," *Krisis and Praxis* (2006), http://www.krisispraxis.com, (accessed, May 3, 2017).

[115] Knitter, *Introducing Theologies of Religions*, 157 - 158.

Furthermore, the consideration of religions as mere phenomenon of the indefinable Reality tends to work against Hick's proposition of religious pluralism that seeks to project and respect religious difference as necessary for unity among religions. Rather, what is noticed is the subordination of the religious traditions under a common ground. In view of this, Marianne Moyaert asserts:

> The Pluralist presupposition of interreligious unity is the claim of religious differences; the latter becomes subordinated to the common ground. Thus, the presupposed commonality between the different religions ends in a homogenization of religious heterogeneity: pluralism wants to bridge the plurality by imposing a unity on the variety.[117]

The differences between the religions are relegated to the background while the universality and commonalities are emphasized. Hick is therefore, accused of failing to adequately consider the fact "that the various religions do not ask the same questions (of salvation), and that religious plurality will not be sublimated in a unified pluralism."[118] Supporting this criticism, Heim argues that religions are different and are geared towards different ends. He contends that "Nirvana and communion with God are contradictory only if we assume that one or the other must

---

[116] S. Mark Heim, *Is Christ the Only Way? Christian Faith in a Pluralistic World* (Valley Forge, PA: Judson, 1985), 144.

[117] Marianne Moyaert, *In Response to the Religious Other: Ricoeur and the Fragility of Interreligious Encounters* (New York: Lexington Books, 2014), 127.

[118] Ibid., 120.

be the sole fate for all human beings."[119] What Heim emphasis here is that what the Buddhist means by enlightenment in a nonpersonal bliss is different from what a Christian understands by eternal union with a loving God. This will make dialogue very difficult because the non-negotiable elements of religions will always pose a challenge in the application of Hick's pluralism in interreligious dialogue.

Although a pluralist, Paul Knitter, aligns with Hick in embracing dialogue from a soteriological stance, he differs slightly by focusing more on this-worldly social transformation in a praxis-oriented approach. According to Knitter, "the absolute that all else must serve and clarify, is not the Church or Christ or even God – but rather, the Kingdom and its justice."[120] Knitter understands the mission of Jesus purely as a mission of modelling toward living the life of the Kingdom. Knitter focusses on social justice rather than individual redemption from sin, following liberationist approach. He observes that:

> [F]ollowers of Jesus would do better off if they understood (and felt) Jesus more as a sacrament of God's love than a satisfaction for God's justice. In the technical language we've already encountered, the way Jesus "saves" – that is, the way he enters people's lives and connect with

---

[119] S. Mark Heim, *Salvations: Truth and difference in Religions* (Maryknoll, N.Y.: Orbis Books, 1995), 149.

[120] Paul F. Knitter, "Toward a Liberation Theology of Religions," in *The Myth of Christian Uniqueness:Toward a Pluralistic Theology of Religions,* eds., John Hick and Paul F. Knitter (New York: Orbis Books, 1987), 190.

God – can be understood better as representative cause rather than a constitutive cause. More simply, Jesus "saves" people not by fixing something but by showing something. He doesn't have to fix or rebuild the bridge between God and humanity by responding to God's demand for satisfaction for humanity's sinfulness. Rather, his task is to reveal or show humanity that God's love is already there, ready to embrace and empower, no matter how often humans have lost their way and narrow-minded.[121]

Furthermore, Knitter advocates for the prioritization of universal ethics and the care of the ecosystem as imperatives for effective interreligious relations, since they are the real issues that impact on people of every creed, rather than doctrinal beliefs.

Knitter proposes that rather than concentrating on the things that divide them, religions should focus their energy on how to defeat their common human challenges. He asks: "If religions do not have any given common ground, don't they have common problems? And all of these problems are focused or fed, one might say, in one reality: suffering."[122] For Knitter, dialogue should adopt a pragmatic approach to the reality of human existence, thus, "the suffering of others becomes mediator, as it were, or conduit of trust and comprehension, between differing religious worlds."[123] According to him, this approach to

---

[121] Knitter, *Introducing Theologies of Religions*, 152-153.

[122] Ibid, 231-232.

[123] Paul Knitter, *One Earth, Many Religions: Multifaith Dialogue and Global Responsibility* (Maryknoll, N.Y.: Orbis Books,

dialogue is more effective, because it addresses not what is within religions but what confronts all religions from outside.[124] It is a global responsibility to the mother earth and its inhabitants. In this approach therefore, the shared anguish of the suffering, physical suffering, socio-economic oppression, nuclear oppression, and ecological disasters become a common ground and context for effective and responsible interreligious dialogue.[125] Concurring to this view, Smith argues: "Christianity is not true absolutely, impersonally, statically; rather, it can become true, if and as we appropriate it to ourselves and interiorize it, insofar as we live it out from day to day. It becomes true as we take it off the shelf and personalize it, in actual existence."[126]

Knitter also proposes a dialogical Christology that is "kingdom-centered" or "regnocentric." A kingdom-centered dialogue will prioritize the promotion of the heart of Jesus' message: the spreading of the reign of God on earth. This is a kingdom of justice, love and peace. This is not a Christology that emphasises the *a priori* understanding of Jesus as the definite revelation but in the praxis of his ministry and teachings on the reign of the Kingdom of God, which is inchoately present in the world.[127] Recognizing that the kingdom of God has a Christian

---

1995), 13.

[124] Paul Knitter, "Making Sense of the Many," *Religious Studies Review* 15, no.3 (1989), 207.

[125] Knitter, "Interreligious Dialogue," 27-30.

[126] Wilfred Cantwell Smith, *Towards a World Theology* (Philadelphia, PA: Westminster 1981), 187.

[127] Paul F. Knitter, "Catholics and Other Religions: Bridging the Gap Between Dialogue and Theology," *Louvain Studies* 24 (1999), 343-344.

denotation, he argues that the kingdom is present wherever the values of the kingdom are promoted. This means that the kingdom extends to non-Christian religions inasmuch as they reflect in their way of life the fruits of the kingdom. In the promotion of the values of the kingdom, all religions will find a common ground and context for effective dialogue. Regnocentric approach to dialogue overcomes triumphalism of considering other religions as finding their fulfilment in Christianity or in the church, but all serving as equal partners.

The major criticism of Knitter's approach relates to his denial of doctrinal criteria for truth and insisting only on ethical criteria. Orthopraxis takes precedence over orthodoxy, and the implication is that it creates false dichotomy between theological propositions as statements on reality on the one hand and subjective experiences or personal values on the other. In view of this, Ratzinger argues that doctrines matter, and they inform practice and conduct. Thus, it is vital to ground ethical judgement of an action within the *a priori* principles of the religion.[128]

Generally, in the context of interreligious dialogue, pluralistic approach aims at overcoming the exclusivist claims on religions that lead to the exclusion of other religions. It does so by creating something shareable by all people and adherents of various religious traditions, which will enhance equality, necessary for dialogue. However, it overlooks or trivializes the irreducible particularity of religions. According to Marianne Moyaert, "Pluralists are

---

[128] Cardinal Joseph Ratzinger, "Relativism: The Central Problem for Faith Today," http://www.ewtn.com/library/CURIA/RATZRELA.htm (accessed April 12, 2017).

so eager to promote dialogue that they overlook the irreducible differences that exists between the religious traditions."[129] Those unique doctrines of religions, when denied or removed, alters the self-understanding of the religion by its adherents. Furthermore, kingdom-centered or Reality-centered lays emphasis on moral principles of a religion, but the interpretation of principles differ according to the historical context and doctrines of religion. The imposition of ones' religious view on other religions, will make dialogue difficult. These objections seem to undermine pluralism as a viable paradigm in interreligious dialogue.

2.4. Inclusivism

In Christian theologies of religion, inclusivism stands as a via media between exclusivism and pluralism. It seeks to find a creative way for effective dialogue among other religion without the denial of the absolute truth claim of the Christian faith. According to Race, inclusivism avoids the perils of absolutism and exclusivism in seeking ways of integrating other religions into Christian theological reflections.[130] To accomplish this goal, it holds together two equally binding convictions: first; that the grace of God operates in all major religions of the world for salvation, and second; the uniqueness of salvation as accomplished in Jesus Christ as universal and as the final way of salvation.[131] In this way, "inclusivism in one hand, opposes the exclusivist position that limits the possibility of salvation to explicit believers in Jesus Christ," and on the other hand, it

---

[129]Moyaert, *In Response to the Religious Other,* 120.
[130] Race, *Christians and Religious Pluralism,* 38.
[131] Ibid.

is in opposition to pluralism's equality of the truth claims of all religions by insisting that Jesus has a genuine role in salvation, which some theologians in this school have described as "absolute," while some others describe as "normative," and (or) "constitutive."[132]

The "fulfillment model" is a position within inclusivism derived from the notion that although grace is present in the religions prompting people to salvation, they can only find the plenitude of salvation in Jesus Christ. Knitter describes the fulfillment model as the recognition that God's love is universal, extending to all peoples, but also that "God's love is particular, made real in Jesus the Christ."[133] The proponents of this model support their notion from some scriptural passages such as: "Truly I perceive that God shows no partiality, but in every nation, anyone who fears him and does what is right is acceptable to him" (Act. 10:35); "In past generations he allowed all nations to walk in their own ways; yet he did not leave himself without witness..." (Acts. 14:16); and Paul's speech at the Areopagus (Act. 17.22-31), where he redirected their worship of the unknown God to the true living God.

---

[132] Mathew G. Minix, "Contemporary Inclusivism: Does God Give and Gather the Traditions?" in *Religious Diversity and the American Experience: A Theological Approach,* eds.Terrence W. Tilley et al (New York:Continuum International Publishing, 2007) 81. In this book, Terrence Tilley and his students classify Inclusivism into Classic and Contemporary. Rahner who was associated with the classic model describes Jesus as the "absolute savior," while Contemporary approaches like those of Gavin D'Costa and Jacques Dupuis describe Jesus as the "Normative and the Constitutive savior" respectively. Explanation of these terms are contained in the next chapter.

[133] Knitter, *Introducing Theologies of Religions*, 63.

As early as the second century, this view was present in the understanding and teachings of some of the fathers of the Church. They explained the presence of God in other religions as *logos spermatikos* or the seed of the word. The logos as Seed or Word of God has been in existence and scattered among peoples even before the incarnation, however, they maintained that the seed-word scattered among cultures and religions needs to be fulfilled or embodied in the word of Jesus Christ.[134] For example, Justin the Martyr teaches that whoever receives God's call in this seed-word and follows its lead is a Christian, even if he never heard of Christ.[135] Interpreting Justin's theology of the *Logos*, Race explains that the understanding of the *logos* in other religion is that it is partial and incomplete compared with the fullness of truth and goodness in Jesus. This means that the *logos* is operative in the other religions to prepare them for the appearance of the *logos* in Christ. Jacque Dupuis, analyzing the theological implications of this teaching, states: "Christianity exists beyond its visible boundaries and prior to its historical appearing, but up to the incarnation, it is fragmentary, hidden, even mixed with error, and ambiguous."[136] Reflecting this view, Tertullian teaches that because of the universal presence and call of God, the spirit of every human being is "naturally Christian."[137]

Another important approach to theological inclusivism is Karl Rahner's concept of "anonymous Christian." This term refers to non-Christians who live a life of love and

---

[134] Cf. Knitter, *Introducing Theologies of Religions*, 65.

[135] Ibid.

[136] Dupuis, *Towards a Christian Theology of Religious,* 60.

[137] Ibid.

truth by obeying the dictates of their consciences within the confines of their religion, therefore, are implicitly Christians. As Rahner explains:

> [T]he anonymous Christian in our sense of the term is the pagan after the beginning of the Christian mission, who lives in the state of Christ's grace through faith, hope and love, yet who has no explicit knowledge of the fact his life is oriented in grace-given salvation to Jesus Christ.[138]

Rahner came to this conviction drawing from two major Christian theological analysis. Firstly, God, who desires all to be saved, cannot consign all non-Christians to hell. Secondly, Jesus Christ is God's only means of salvation. It then means that the non-Christians who make it to heaven must have received the grace of Christ without their realizing it. The goal of this teaching is to resolve "the polar tension between the claims of the necessity of the Christian faith for salvation and the acknowledgement of the universal salvific will of God's love and power."[139]

The Second Vatican Council has been described as the watershed in the Roman Catholic Church's approach to the religions of the world because it epitomizes the inclusivist paradigm, deeply exploring the idea of the universality of God's salvation for all people as it is made particular in the incarnation, death and resurrection of Jesus. The "Dogmatic Constitution on the Church" (*Lumen Gentium*)

---

[138] Karl Rahner, *Theological Investigation* 14, trans., David Bourke (London: Darton, Logman and Todd 1976), 28.

[139] Gavin D'Costa, "Karl Rahner Anonymous Christian – A Reappraisal," *Modern Theology* 1 no.2 (January 1985), 131-148.

#13 states: "finally all humankind are called by God's grace to salvation." In the same vein #16 specifies religious affiliation and extending it to those with no faith:

> Those to whom the covenants, and from whom Christ was born in the flesh, those who acknowledge the creator, first among who are Muslims, those who, through no fault of their own, do not know the Gospel of Christ or his church, but who nevertheless seek God with sincere heart, those who without any fault of theirs, have not yet arrived at an explicit knowledge of God, and who without grace, strive to lead a good life.[140]

The Council based its decision on two New Testament passages: Acts 17:25-28; "He gives life and breath to all things," and 1 Tim 2:4; "and since the Savior wills everyone to be saved."

The Vatican II Council's inclusive approach highlights these elements: the universal presence of the Spirit among peoples, cultures and religions; that invincible ignorance exonerates those who live life of love and truth, but because of no fault of theirs could not come to explicit faith in Christ; the recognition of implicit faith among non-Christians who live the life of grace; and that whatever is

---

[140]Catholic Church, "Dogmatic Constitution on the Church" - *Lumen Gentium,*
http://www.vatican.va/archive/hist_councils/ii_vatican_council/docume nts/vat-ii_const_19641121_lumen-gentium_en.html(accessed April 30, 2017). Subsequent quotations from this document will be taken from this website, and to be cited as *Lumen Gentium.*

good in the religions are rays of truth that need to be brought to the true light of faith.

First, as the "Pastoral Constitution on the Church in the Modern World" (*Gaudium et Spes*), points out, "the Spirit offers to all the possibility of being made partners in a way known only to God, in the paschal mystery."[141] This assertion corresponds with Rahner's "anonymous Christians" by recognizing the implicit presence of the Spirit of Christ in other religions without explicit reference to Christ. Article 41 declares that the Spirit of God will always arouse the heart of men and women of every age that they will never be indifferent to religion.[142] Similarly, the "Decree on the Mission Activity of the Church" (*Ad Gentes*), dwells profoundly on the activity of the Spirit in other religions. The document points out that the Spirit was at work in the world before Christ.[143] It acknowledges elements of truth and goodness, which are found among religions and peoples as a secret presence of God.[144] It further affirms the generous gift, which God has distributed

---

[141]Catholic Church, "Pastoral Constitution on the Church in the Modern World" – *Gauduim et Spes*, http://www.vatican.va/archive/hist_councils/ii_vatican_council/docume nts/vat-ii_cons_19651207_gaudium-et-spes_en.html(accessed April 30, 2017),no. 22. Subsequent quotes from this document will be taken from this website, and will be cited as *Gauduin et Spes*.

[142] GS, 41.

[143] Catholic Church,"Degree on the Mission Activity of the Church" – *Ad Gentes*, http://www.vatican.va/archive/hist_councils/ii_vatican_council/docume nts/vat-ii_decree_19651207_ad-gentes_en.html(accessed, April 30, 2017), no. 4. Subsequent quotes from this document will be taken from this website, and will be cited as *Ad Gentes*.

[144]*Ad Gentes*, no.9.

among the nations.[145] The Conciliar document, "Declaration on the Relation of the Church to non-Christian Religion"(*Nostra Aetate*), indicates that the church rejects nothing of what is good and true in other religions.[146] They reflect a ray of that truth which enlightens all.[147] Christians are encouraged to seek out the spiritual and moral truths found in other religions.[148] This implies that despite the call to dialogue with other religions the evangelizing/missionary mandate of the church is sacrosanct.

Second, the condition of invincible ignorance and implicit faith are adopted in the conciliar documents also as reasons for the possibility of salvation among people who live in shadows and images and seek the unknown God.[149] This includes those who, through no fault of theirs, do not know the gospel of Christ and of his church and those who, without blame on their part have not yet arrived at explicit knowledge of God.[150] Furthermore, the Vatican II identifies the human heart or conscience as the place of divine encounter and affirms that even in invincible ignorance, people who follow the voice of God deep in their hearts in seeking to do his will not be denied salvation (Act 10:35).[151]

---

[145] Ibid., no.11.

[146]*Nostra Aetate*, no.2.

[147] Ibid., no.2.

[148] Ibid.

[149] Thomas Aquinas describes invincible ignorance (*invincibilis*) as not voluntary. Such that a person cannot overcome by diligence. Thus, the individual is not culpable. Cf. Thomas Aquinas, *Summa Theologiae* vol. 25: Sin(1a2ae.71 – 80), trans. and ed. John Fearon (London Blackfrairs, 1969), 148.

[150]*Lumen Gentium*, no.16.

[151] Ibid, no. 9.

However, this is inspired by grace through ways known to God alone. The *Ad Gentes* clearly explains: "So, although in ways known to himself God can lead those who, through no fault of their own, are ignorant of the gospel to that faith without which it is impossible to please him."[152] In addition, the idea of mysterious working of God's grace in the hearts of non-Christians for salvation corresponds with the teachings of the Catechism of Catholic Church: "God has bound salvation to the sacrament of baptism, but he himself is not bound by the sacrament."[153]

From the foregoing exposition of positive salvific posture of the council for those of other religion, however, the Council is insisting that grace is not simply available to all implicitly and in saving ways without the explicit priority placed on the gospel. *Lumen Gentium* lucidly states: "whatever of good or truth is found amongst them is considered by the church to be a preparation for the gospel."[154] Stressing the necessity of the mission of the church, *Ad Gentes* explains that it aims to "purge of evil association those elements of truth and grace which are found among peoples, and which are, as it were, a secret presence of God; and it restores them to Christ their source who overthrows the rule of the devil and limits the manifold malice of evil."[155] This idea is reiterated in *Ad Gentes*, "these efforts need to be enlightened and corrected,

---

[152]*Ad Gentes*, 7.

[153] Catholic Church, *Catechism of the Catholic Church: With Modifications from the Editio Typica* (Toronto: Image Book Doubleday, 1995), no.1257.

[154]*Lumen Gentium*, no.16.

[155]*Ad Gentes*, no.9.

although in loving providence of God they may lead one to the true God and be a preparation for the gospel."[156]

Similarly, *Nostra Aetate* highlights this view, but goes further to attribute the "seed of the word" to the whole corpus of their religions.[157] This is significant because it seemingly gives affirmation to the internal mechanism and elements of a religious tradition. The Council fathers see these elements as preparation for the gospel and so urge Christians to be faithful in proclaiming Jesus Christ, the true light that enlightens all men and women: "Proclaim Christ who is the Way, the Truth and the Life (Jn 1:6). In whom God reconciled all things to himself (2Cor 5:18-19), people find the fullness of their religious life."[158] The conciliar document exhorts Christians to engage in interreligious dialogue with non-Christian religions, and to "acknowledge, preserve and encourage the spiritual and moral truths found among non-Christians."[159] It seems clear that the Council fathers took an inclusivist stance, a positive openness through the affirmation of implicit faith in the heart of non-Christians. However, the document insist that truth reflected in other religions is only a preparation for the gospel. Truth in other traditions are to be purified through evangelization.

As positive as it may seem, the teachings of Vatican II embody tensions that raised few theological controversies. The first is the implication of article 7 of *Ad Gentes*, which states that there is mediation of grace in the heart of those who, while not knowing Christ do the will of God. God

---

[156] Ibid., 3.
[157] *Nostra Aetate*, no.2.
[158] Ibid., no.2
[159] Ibid.

grants the grace for such action through ways known alone to him (God). Some theologians interpret this as an argument against the sole or unique mediation of salvation in Christ. Thus, God can mediate salvation through alternative sources since these people do not profess Christian faith.[160]

Secondly, *Nostra Aetate*'s affirmation of "ray of truth," of things "good and holy" in other religions seemingly supports the argument for equality of religious truth. This could imply that one religion is considered as good as the other, a position tantamount to the pluralist approach discussed above. These issues have dominated theological discussions since the Post-Conciliar era and have raised more questions about the role of dialogue in relation to proclamation in the mission of the church.

Some of the Post-Conciliar popes have contributed to the discussion. I will briefly highlight some of the contributions of Paul VI and John Paul II. Paul VI's Apostolic Exhortation "On the Proclamation of the Gospel in the World" (*EvangeliiNuntiandi*), devoted article 53 to non-Christian religions by advancing the attitude of deep respect that the church has for religious values of these religions.[161]

---

[160] Theologians like Jacques Dupuis argues that Jesus is unique not in the absolute or relative sense, but in the constitutive and relational sense. By constitutive he implies that the paschal mystery has a universal significance for Christians. A privileged way by which God extends his salvation to people. By relational, he means that there is a reciprocal relationship by the way of Jesus and the other religions. Therefore, the implication is that the universal salvation in Jesus does not deny or contradict the saving significance of other religions. Dupuis, *Toward a Christian Theology of Religious Pluralism*, 305-307.

[161] Pope Paul VI, Apostolic Exhortation"-*Evangelii Nuntiandi*,

Furthermore, relating these religions with Christianity, Paul VI avers that the other religions should come to the true fulfillment of their search for God in the Christian faith. He argues that "our religion effectively establishes with God an authentic and living relationship which the other religions do not succeed in doing even though they have, as it were, their arms stretched out towards heaven."[162] As such, Paul VI insists that the church has the obligation to "give witness before them of the fullness of the revelation whose deposit she guards."[163]

On his part, Pope John Paul II deepens the teachings of the Second Vatican Council about the activities of the Spirit beyond the confines of the church. John Paul II developed this theological position in three magisterial documents; *Redemptor Hominis, Dominum et Vivificantem* and *Redemptoris Missio*.[164]

In *Redemptor Hominis*, John Paul II encouraged dialogue with non-Christian religions by acknowledging the human and spiritual treasures in them. He asserts that they are "effects of the Spirit of truth operating outside the

---

http://w2.vatican.va/content/paul-vi/en/apost_exhortations/documents/hf_p-vi_exh_19751208_evangelii-nuntiandi.html (accessed December 20, 2017), no.53. Subsequent quotations from this document will be taken from this website, and will be cited as *Evangelii Nuntiandi*.

[162] Ibid.

[163] Ibid.

[164] According to Gerlad O'Collins, Pope John Paul II's contributions towards advancing pneumateological arguments for interreligious dialogue is profound that he fittingly could be addressed as the Vicar of the Holy Spirit, just as he is called the Vicar of Christ. Gerlad O'Collins, "John Paul II on Christ, the Holy Spirit, and World Religions," *Irish Theological Quarterly* 72 (2007):330.

visible confines of the church."[165] This affirmation cautions Christians against wavering in faith on discovering such wonders in other religions.[166] In article 11 of *Redemptor Hominis*, the pope echoed Vatican II's deep esteem for the great spiritual values in other religions, he considers them as "seed of the word." and preparation for evangelization. In furtherance of his theological reflection on the universal activity of the Spirit, John Paul II in *Dominum et Vivificantem*, explores the "actions of the Holy Spirit even before Christ – from the beginning, throughout the world, and especially in the economy of the Old Covenant."[167] He recognizes the action of the Spirit in every place, time and people according to the eternal plan of God, and directed towards salvation in Christ.[168]

In *RedemptorisMissio*, he maintains that the activity of the Holy Spirit is special in the Church, and asserts that it is "universal, limited neither by space nor time."[169] It is

---

[165] Pope John Paul II, "Redemptor Hominis: An Encyclical letter," http://w2.vatican.va/content/john-paul-ii/en/encyclicals/documents/hf_jp-ii_enc_04031979_redemptor-hominis.html(accessed December 21, 2016), no.6.

[166] Ibid.

[167] Pope John Paul II, "Dominum et Vivificantem: On the Holy Spirit in the Life of the Church and the World," 53http://w2.vatican.va/content/john-paul-ii/en/encyclicals/documents/hf_jp-ii_enc_18051986_dominum-et-vivificantem.html (accessed December 21, 2017), no.53.

[168] Ibid.

[169] Pope John Paul II, "Redemptoris Missio: On the Permanent Validity of the Church's Missionary Mandate," http://w2.vatican.va/content/john-paul-ii/en/encyclicals/documents/hf_jp-ii_enc_07121990_redemptoris-missio.html (accessed December 21, 2017), no. 28. Subsequent quotations from this document will be taken from this website, and will

present in the form of "seed of the word" in individuals and manifested in initiatives and in human "efforts to attain truth, goodness and God himself."[170] Therefore, by engaging in dialogue the Church seeks to uncover the "seeds of the Word, a "ray of that truth which enlightens all men" found in individuals and in the religious traditions of the world.[171] The action of the Spirit has a social effect because it affects society and history, people, cultures and religions.[172] The pope believes that the Holy Spirit prompts every authentic prayer, signaling to his call for World Day of Prayer.[173] In *RedemptorisMissio*John Paul II stresses the unique and universal salvific mediation in Christ, but recognizes the possibility of participatory forms of mediations of salvation. He claims: "Although participated forms of mediation of different kinds and degrees are not excluded, they acquire meaning and value only from Christ's own mediation, and they cannot be understood as parallel or complementary to His."[174] The idea of participatory mediation has continued to provoke ongoing theological discussions.[175] John Paul II has through pneumatological approach to dialogue, brought about more openness to the Church's relations with other worldreligions.[176]

---

be cited as *Redemptoris Missio.*

[170] Ibid

[171] Ibid., no.56.

[172] Ibid., no.28, 29.

[173] Ibid

[174] Ibid., no.5.

[175]This theological position of Pope John Paul II is explored by Jacques Dupuis and advanced to propose his controversial Christian theology of religious pluralism. This will be examined in the next chapter.

2.5. Conclusion

In conclusion, this chapter critically examined Race's tripod model in the theology of religions and identified inclusivism as the preferred position of the Roman Catholic Church in her relationship with other religions. The foregoing discussion reveals that through their teachings, the Council fathers and the popes promulgated inclusivism as a theological position of the Church, which aims to acknowledge the salvific will of God for all people and its fulfillment in Christ. Vatican II hoped that this could be a step forward towards dialogical openness. The next chapter evaluates the effectiveness of inclusivism in dialogue between Islam and Christianity by comparing the works of selected theologians from both religions.

---

[176] The contributions of the subsequent papacies of Pope Benedict XVI and Pope Francis will be highlighted within the body of this work.

Chapter Three

Comparing Inclusivism in Christianity and Islam

3.1. Introduction

Building from the discussion in the last chapter, this chapter explores the theologies of some selected contemporary theologians from Christianity and Islam in the light of inclusivism. It involves an analysis of how inclusivist categories of the two traditions could facilitate effective dialogical experience in their relationship. From the Christian religion, I will briefly investigate the works of two theologians; Gavin D'Costa and Jacques Dupuis. Although both theologians are distinct in their theological formulations, their theologies embody the core principles of inclusivism. From Islamic religion, I will analyze the works of Reza Shah-Kazemi and Amir Hussein members of Ismaili and Sunni sects respectively. My point is not to advocate one or another author's positions, but rather to show how they present viable expressions of inclusivism and offer resources for dialogue.

My examination of the two Muslim theologians develops from a twofold rationale. First, since Christians and Muslims dominate the Nigerian religious terrain, an exposition such as this one will provide an orientation for Catholic interlocutors to look for analogous principles within Islam that can open prospects for effective dialogue. Second, the discussion will show how inclusivism exists in non-Christian traditions like Islam, exploring it as an Islamic middle-way between exclusivist and pluralist approaches. Hence, this chapter tries to present inclusivism found in the works of these thinkers as a foundation for interreligious dialogical praxis in Christian-Muslim relations in Nigeria.

3.2. Gavin D'Costa: Trinitarian Theology and other Religions

Gavin D'Costa is a prominent Roman Catholic theologian, outstanding in Christian Theology of Religions, with numerous literatures and articles on interreligious dialogue to his record. D'Costa's major contribution to this field is the application of Trinitarian theology as the basis for effective dialogue with world religions. Opposing both extremes of exclusivism and pluralism as theologically untenable and ineffective in dialogue with other religions, he makes the case for the Trinitarian theology of religions. This is because Trinitarian theology holds together the particularity of salvation in Christ, and the universality of God's love through the Spirit for all people, cultures and religions. He summarizes his Trinitarian theology and its effectiveness as follow:

> [T]he doctrine seeks to affirm that God has disclosed himself unreservedly and irreversibly in the contingencies and particularities of the person Jesus. But within Trinitarian thinking we are also able to affirm in the action of the third person, that God is constantly revealing himself through history by means of the Holy Spirit. The Spirit in the activity serves to deepen and universalize our understanding of God in Christ, a process that is incomplete until parousia.[177]

This passage encapsulates the crux of D'Costa's Trinitarian theology of religions. Noteworthy, is the interplay of

---

[177] Gavin D'Costa, "Towards a Trinitarian Theology of Religions," *A Universal Faith?: Peoples, Cultures, Religions and the Christ: Essays in Honor of Prof. Dr. Frank De Graeve*, eds., Catherine Cornille and Valeer Neckebrouck (Louvain: W. B. Eerdmans, 1992), 147.

Christology and Pneumatology in the development of a theological dialectics between particularity and universality.

D'Costa outlined five theses for his Trinitarian theology of religions in the book, *Christian Uniqueness Reconsidered: The Myth of a Pluralistic Theology of Religions*. They include:

- A Trinitarian Christology guards against classical exclusivism and pluralism by dialectically relating the universal and the particular.
- Pneumatology [sic] allows the particularity of Christ to be related to the universal activity of God in the history of humankind.
- A Christocentric Trinitarianism discloses loving relationship as the proper mode of being. Hence, love of neighbor (which includes Hindus, Buddhist, Muslims, and others, especially in a pluralistic society and a globalized world) is an imperative for all Christians.
- The normativity of Christ involves the normativity of crucified self-giving love.
- The church stands under the judgment of the Holy Spirit, and if the Holy Spirit is active in the world religions, then the world religions are vital to Christian faithfulness.[178]

In the following sections, I will briefly examine the principles behind these theses in relation to dialogue with religions under the classifications: Trinitarian Christology, Trinitarian pneumatology and Trinitarian ecclesiology.

---

[178] Gavin D'Costa, "Christ, the Trinity and Religious Plurality" *Christian Uniqueness Reconsidered: The Myth of a Pluralistic Theology of Religions*, ed., G. D'Costa (New York: Orbis, 1990), 16-29

3.2.1. Trinitarian Christology

According to D'Costa, the Triune God is encountered in its fullness in Christ through the Spirit.[179] The revelation of God is thus a collective action of the Son and the Spirit. He states that it is "through Christ that we encounter a Trinitarian God, who makes himself known as he is: as an utter and gracious mystery (God the Father), in the Word Incarnate (God the Son), and in God's indwelling sanctifying and prophetic presence (the Spirit)"[180] It is important to note his deliberate avoidance of the ascription of revelation of God exclusively to Jesus Christ, which invariably leads to christomonism.[181] He argues that Jesus is to be regarded as *totus Deus*, but never "*totumdeum*; wholly God, but never the whole God."[182] The description of the inner working of the Trinity as *perichoresis*, which means that the three co-inhere, resonates aptly in D'Costa's analysis of the Trinity. He describes Jesus as the normative revelation of God, in contrast to Karl Rahner's description of Christ as the absolute savior.[183] Christ's normativity implies that whatever is revealed or known about God cannot contradict what is known through Christ.[184] Referencing George Lindbeck he quotes: "Whatever is said of the Father is said of the Son, except that the Son is not the Father." This assertion eschews an "exclusive identification of God and Jesus as well as a non-normative identification of God and Jesus."[185]

---

[179] Ibid.

[180] Ibid., 17.

[181]Ibid., 18.

[182] Ibid., 18-19.

[183] Karl Rahner considers Christ and Christianity as the absolute religion, which is intended for all peoples, and "which cannot recognize any other religion besides itself of equal right." Karl Rahner, *Theological Investigations*, vol. 5 (London: Longman and Todd, 1966), 118.

[184] D'Costa, "Towards A Trinitarian Theology of Religion," 149.

The normativity of Christ is not static. Our understanding of God could only be fully reached at the *eschaton*. Our understanding is "constantly transformed and enriched through the guiding/declaring/judging function of the Spirit."[186] In other words, revelation is "Christologically determined," and anything defined apart from Christ is not in accordance with "Christian understanding of revelation."[187] However, this does not mean that we cannot discover new things about God, or that God cannot surprise us. Instead, it means that, whatever is newly discovered is to be ontologically related to Christ, because the economic Trinity is the immanent Trinity.[188] In view of that, D'Costa avers:

> However, by saying a priori that there is no new revelation apart from Christ, one is neither circumscribing nor restricting the reality of the Holy Spirit's universal and particular activity, or limiting it exclusively to previous practices and understandings within the living tradition. The statement that there is no new revelation is a claim that all truth, in whatever form, will serve to make Christ known more fully to Christians - (and to world?)[189]

He believes that the space between Jesus and the *eschaton*, give us the opportunity to listen to what God reveals through the Spirit in the religions.

---

[185] Ibid.

[186] Ibid., 152. Gavin D'Costa, "A Christian Reflection on Some Problems with Discerning 'God' in the World Religions," *Dialogue and Alliance 5* (1991),13.

[187] D'Costa, "Revelation and World Religions," 134, 136.

[188] D'Costa, *The Meeting of Religions and the Trinity*, 38.

[189] Ibid., 129.

3.2.2. Trinitarian Pneumatology

The orientation to the Trinity, according to D'Costa, "facilitates an openness to the world's religions for the activity of the Spirit cannot be confined to Christianity."[190] Relying heavily on the trajectories of Conciliar and Post-Conciliar documents, he affirms the presence of the Spirit's activity in other religions. He argues that article 22 of *Gadium et Spes* maintains the possibility of linking the paschal mystery in a universal way through the Spirit. Therefore, the Spirit's presence in other religions elevates them to a potentially dialogue partners.[191] The union of the three persons of the Trinity is a union of love. It is a love that overflows and invites us into loving relationship with others.[192]

D'Costa considers the presence of the Spirit in other religions as an invitation to "relational engagement."[193] Explaining further this, he states: "Through the Spirit, God's Trinitarian presence within other religions and cultures is a possibility, and one that is discerned by signs of the kingdom inchoately present within that culture."[194] He urges the church to be attentive to the presence of the Spirit in other religions, because failing to do so is tantamount to inattentiveness to the word of God entrusted to the Spirit. Thus, D'Costa cautions

---

[190] D'Costa, "Towards A Trinitarian Theology of Religions," 147.

[191] Gavin D'Costa, "Nostra Aetate – Telling God's Story in Asia: Promises and Pitfalls," in *Vatican II and its Legacy*, eds., M. Lamberigts and L. Kenis (Leuven: Leuven University Press, 2002), 336.

[192] Gavin D'Costa, "Revelation and Revelations: Discerning God in Other Religions. Beyond a Static Valuation," *Modern Theology* 10, no.2 (1994), 175.

[193] Gavin D'Costa, *The Meeting of the Religions and the Trinity*, 109.

[194] Ibid., 114.

that, "if the Spirit is at work in the religions, then the gifts of the Spirit need to be discovered, fostered and received into the church. If the church fails to be receptive, it may be unwittingly practicing cultural and religious idolatry."[195]

3.2.3. Trinitarian Ecclesiology

D'Costa's Trinitarian theology of religions is inseparably bound up with the church. Veli Matti Karkkainen notes that, the introduction of ecclesiology into Trinitarian theology through the action of the Spirit is the unique contributions of D'Costa to Theology of Religion.[196] Explaining the Trinitarian foundation of the church, and its relations to other religions, D'Costa states:

> [W]herever God is present, this is the presence of the triune God; and it is this triune God who is the foundation of the Church [...] the Holy Spirit's presence within other religions is both intrinsically Trinitarian and ecclesiological. It is Trinitarian in referring the Holy Spirit's activity to the paschal mystery of Christ, and ecclesial in referring the paschal event to the constitutive community-creating force it has, under the guidance of the Spirit.[197]

D'Costa further develops his Trinitarian ecclesiology by analyzing the similarities and differences in the activity of the Spirit prior to the first coming of Christ and after Pentecost. He

---

[195] Ibid., 115.

[196] Veli Matti Karkkainen, *Trinity and Religious Pluralism: The Doctrine of the Trinity in Christian Theology of Religions* (Aldershot, London: England, 2004), 69-70.

[197] D'Costa, *The Meeting of the Religions and the Trinity*, 110.

argues that "there are degrees to the work of the Spirit before Christ; and there is a decisive new event at Pentecost."[198] In both "moments," the activities of the Spirit are oriented towards Christ. Prior to the advent of Christ, the Spirit was universally active preparing people for the coming of Christ. This was carried out through the covenantal relationship between God and Israel in the Old Testament. After the coming of Christ, the work of the Spirit consists in "applying the fruits of Christ to people."[199] The church is formed through the application of these fruits, by transforming the life of the believer, to be "Christ-like," and making them partakers in the life of the Trinity. Therefore, "the Spirit within the church has the role of helping the church to follow Christ more truthfully, and coming to indwell the trinity more completely."[200]

Regarding the activity of the Spirit outside the Church, D'Costa avers that the Spirit plays an analogous role in making men and women Christ-like. For him, this ought to form the real Trinitarian basis for the Christians' openness towards other religions. He argues that "the church must be attentive to the possibility of God's gift of himself through the prayers, practices, insights, and traditions found within other religions." Pointing out the significance of Trinitarian ecclesiology, D'Costa emphasizes the need for the church to be attentive to the religions of the world, "otherwise it willfully closes itself to the spirit of truth, which it requires to remain faithful to the truth and be guided by it."[201] The affirmation of the activity of the Spirit outside the church, however, exposes the church to

---

[198] Gavin D'Costa, "The Holy Spirit and the World Religions," *Louvain Studies* 34 (2010), 279-311.

[199] Ibid., 291.

[200] D'Costa, *The Meeting of the Religions and the Trinity*, 115.

[201] D'Costa, "Christian Uniqueness Reconsidered," 23.

vulnerability, because the Spirit may call the church into question in ways that cannot be predicted *a priori*. The other religions could as well help reveal the false ideologies and distorted narrative practices of Christian communities.

Despite being commended for its openness to greater desire for mutual interreligious transformation, D'Costa's theology of religions is reluctant about seeing other religions as vehicles of salvation.[202] He maintains that there is no evidence to suggest that the Roman Catholic Church considers other religions *per se* as vehicle of salvation for its members. According to D'Costa, the silence of the Conciliar and Post-Conciliar documents in affirming other religious structures as mediators of supernatural revelation and salvific grace, should not be construed as leaving the door open for theological affirmative interpretation. Rather, given the truth of the gospel, which reveals Jesus as the normative savior and true revelation of God, he considers it an intentional silence.[203]

Albeit being technically inclusivist, D'Costa's theology of religions leans toward exclusivism. This explains why Hedges categorizes D'Costa among the theologians he regards as 'particularists.'[204] Theological particularism is characterized by postliberal and postmodern outlook; rejecting rationalist and egalitarian tendencies of pluralism, which is perceived as contrary to Christian self-understanding. Although, particularism according to Hedges, advocates respect for differences and attention to particularities of religions, there is a major interest in safeguarding the uniqueness of Christianity,

---

[202] Minix, "Contemporary Inclusivism," 84.

[203] D'Costa, The Meeting of the Religions and the Trinity, 104-105.

[204] Paul Hedges, "Particularities," *Christian Approaches to other Faiths*, eds. P. Hedges and A. Race (London: SCM Press, 2008), 112 - 135.

which cannot be understood as one religion among many without undermining fundamental Christian claims. Abraham Velez de Cea, describes particularists as advocates of a subtle form of exclusivism. According to him, "this new and intellectually more sophisticated form of exclusivism is not necessarily rooted in arrogance, disrespect and ignorance of other religions, but rather on humility, respect and awareness of differences."[205] On this note, Race observes that D'Costa aligns with other inclusivists in viewing other traditions as "valid contexts of the work of the Spirit but ultimately subordinate to the Christian experience of Christ."[206]

In summation, it would be wrong to categorize D'Costa as an exclusivist without qualification; ironically, he does not consider himself an inclusivist either.[207] Based on our usage of

---

[205] Abraham Velez de Cea, "Comparative Theology of Religions and the Typology Exclusivisms-Inclusivisms-Pluralisms," in *Twenty-First Century Theologies of Religions: Retrospection and Future Prospects*, eds., E. J Harris, P. Hedges, and S. Hettiarachchi (Boston: Brill Rodopi, 2013), 34-35.

[206] Alan Race, Interfaith Encounter, 119.

[207] D'Costa, launches several criticisms against inclusivism. He argues that although the inclusivist affirms some elements as good and true in another tradition, the significance of the affirmation for the inclusivist might be quite different what is given in its original tradition. He avers that tradition is an organic whole, therefore, if the inclusivist only chooses some elements of the tradition of the other and reinterpret them just to correspond or fit well to the inclusivist's tradition, it could not rightly be called an affirmation. Hence, he proposes a Trinitarian Christology which according to him is able to offer an account of openness, tolerance and equality that are doctrinally plausible, socially realistic, and rhetorically attractive. D'Costa believes that his approach establishes a Trinitarian orientation to the question of other religions which is neither pluralist nor inclusivist, but both open and faithfully committed to its tradition-specific way of narrating the world. See D'Costa, *Meeting of Religions and the Trinity*, 22 – 23, 138.

Race's tripod paradigm, D'Costa's Trinitarian Christology is an inclusivist theology that is defensive of Christian orthodoxy. More importantly, D'Costa's approach is open toward dialogical engagement with other faiths, encouraging *a posteriori* rather than *a priori* judgement.[208] Next, I will examine another contemporary inclusivist theologian who inclines towards pluralism.

3.3. Jacques Dupuis: Trinitarian Theology and Inclusive Pluralism

Jacques Dupuis was born in Belgium in 1923, joined the Jesuits and was ordained a priest in 1954. From 1960-1984 he worked as a missionary in India. In 1984, he became a professor of Christology at the Pontifical Gregorian University in Rome. He served as an advisor to the Pontifical Council for Interreligious Dialogue. In 1997, he published his controversial *magnus opus* entitled, *Towards a Christian Theology of Religious Pluralism*. The book as Dupuis describes it, engages in an "organic and synthetic way of dealing with the reality of religious plurality," with the hope to "maintain Christian identity while being committed to interfaith dialogue and conversion."[209] He analyzes the trends in Christian theology of religions, which he regards as paradigm shifts from ecclesiocentrism, to christocentrism and finally to theocentric pluralism. Based on his analysis of the trend, Dupuis proposes a Trinitarian theology of religious pluralism, or what he later called "inclusive pluralism" as the effective approach towards Christians' relations with world religions. According to Dupuis:

---

[208] D'Costa, "Revelation and Revelations," 168-169.

[209] Dupuis, *Towards a Christian Theology of Religious Pluralism,* 4.

[W]hereas inclusive Christocentrism is nonnegotiable for Christian theology, it can be combined with a true theocentric pluralism, both aspects being complementary in a single reality. We are accordingly seeking an 'inclusive pluralism' (or 'pluralist inclusivism') model of the theology of religions.[210]

Dupuis' goal in his theology of religions is to take a little step beyond Christocentric inclusivism, by bringing into creative tension, two opposing positions or dialectic; theocentric pluralism and Christocentric inclusivism.[211] In what follows, I will briefly examine, how he tried to achieve this and its implication in Christian dialogue with religions.

3.3.1. Jesus Christ in the Trinity

Dupuis' Christology has its foundation on the doctrine of the Trinity, and "places in full relief the interpersonal relationship between Jesus and God whom he calls Father (Abba), on the one side, and between Jesus and the Spirit whom he will send, on the other."[212] He differentiates between the Christology of "God-man," which he considers to be abstract or "Christology from above" because it is about the personal identity of Jesus as the "only begotten Son," or "preexisting Son of God," and the Christology from below, of "Son-of-God-made-man-in-history," which starts from the human Jesus and his historic event.[213] On one hand, the

---

[210] Jacques Dupuis, *Christianity and the Religions: From Confrontation to Dialogue*(Maryknoll, NY: Orbis Books, 2002), 90.

[211] Ibid., 91.

[212] Ibid., 90.

[213] Ibid.

Christology from above affirms the Christological ontological person of Jesus as the only begotten Son, the incarnate Word of God. On the other hand, the Christology from below anchors on the "functional level." These two Christological theories are related respectively to exclusivism and pluralism. The former insists on the necessity of the mediation of Jesus Christ (1 Tim 2:5), while the latter focuses on the universal salvific will of God (1 Tim 2:4). To ensure a theology that will hold in creative tension both the high and the low Christology, making it open to world religions, Christology must be interpreted through the prism of the personal intra-Trinitarian relations that informs the Christological mystery.

Expounding on the intra-Trinitarian relations, beginning with the relationship between the Father and the Son, Dupuis states: "the unique closeness existing between God and Jesus by the virtue of the mystery of the incarnation may never be forgotten, but neither can the unbridgeable distance that remain between the Father and Jesus in his human existence."[214]Precis ely, what this means is that Jesus is never to be thought as replacing God. Hence, Dupuis teaches that "Jesus is the way, the truth, and the life" (Jn 16:6), he is "never the goal or the end."[215]   This teaching aligns slightly with D'Costa's Christology which considers Jesus Christ as 'wholly God' and never 'the whole of God.'[216] Yet unlike Dupuis, D'Costa does not separate Jesus the only begotten Son of God from the historic Jesus. This means that there is an intra-Trinitarian inseparability existing among the three persons of the Trinity in D'Costa's theology.[217]   Dupuis, however, argues that God is

---

[214] Ibid., 92.

[215] Ibid.

[216] D'Costa, "Christ, the Trinity and Religious Plurality,"18-19.

[217] Ibid.

the absolute mystery, and the source and center of all reality, when understood within the context of God's dealing with humankind. Furthermore, Jesus in his human form is contingent and although he is the unique Son of God, God stands beyond him.[218]

Dupuis' Trinitarian Christology emphasizes that an "integral Christology" requires the Spirit component in all situations, essentially in the development of the Christian theology of religious pluralism. He recognizes the shift in theology of religion from Christ-centered to Word-centered(logocentric) and Spirit-centered(pneumatocentric). The two are the two wings of God through history in the economy of salvation. The scriptures reveal the activity of the Word, all through human history. As the prologue of St. John's gospel indicates, "in the beginning is the Word" (John 1:1-4). He is the "true light that enlightens every human being" (John 1:9). It is the same Word that took flesh at the incarnation. Dupuis concludes that, "in all circumstances, it is the word of God who saves, not precisely the Word-of-God-made-flesh, that is Jesus Christ."[219] However, Dupuis maintains that Jesus Christ, "the incarnate Word," remains the center of God's plan of salvation and of its unfolding history. In effect, "logocentrism and Christocentrism are not mutually opposed; they call to each other in a unique dispensation."[220]

Furthermore, Dupuis argues that Christological pneumatology or the Christology of the Spirit highlights the relationship of Jesus and the Spirit. This is necessary "in order

---

[218] Dupuis, *Christianity and the Religions: From Confrontation to Dialogue*, 92.

[219] Dupuis, *Towards a Christian Theology of Religious Pluralism*, 195.

[220] Ibid., 195.

to avoid the blind alley, a narrow Christocentric perspective necessarily leads to, there is need for a new theology of religions built on a pneumatocentric model."[221] This is because, while the economy of the Christ-event is limited by a particular history, the economy of the spirit, knows no constraint, for the Spirit "blows wherever it wills" (John 3:8). Dupuis notes that the Spirit of God has been active throughout human history and is still active today in the religions of the world, inspiring their adherents to obedience to their faith. He, thus, suggests that it could be that "while Christians secure salvation through the economy of God's Son incarnate in Jesus Christ, others receive it through the immediate autonomous action of the Spirit of God."Linking other religions and people to the Paschal Mystery of Christ, Dupuis argues:

> [T]hrough the power of the Spirit, the Jesus Christ-event is being actuated through all time; it is present and active in every generation. In all cases the immediate influence of the Spirit gives expression to the operative presence of God's saving action which has come to a climax in Jesus Christ.[222]

Dupuis surmises that Christology and pneumatology cannot be interpreted as two distinct and different economies of God's dealings with humankind. They complement each other in a single divine economy. Nevertheless, their functions are distinct. He contends that "the Christ event is at the center of the historical unfolding of the divine economy, but the punctual event of Jesus Christ is actuated and becomes operative throughout time and space in the work of the Spirit."[223]

---

[221] Ibid., 196.

[222] Ibid., 197.

[223] Dupuis, *Christianity and the Religions*, 93.

3.3.2. De Facto and De Jure

Dupuis considers religious pluralism not as an obstacle to be removed, but rather a richness to be celebrated. Re-invoking the question posed by Edward Schillebeeckx about "whether the pluralism of religions is a matter of fact or a matter of principle,"[224] Dupuis in positive affirmation asserts that it is both a matter of fact (de facto), and must be accepted in principle (de jure) because it flows from "the superabundant richness and diversity of God's self-manifestation to humankind." In other words, Dupuis considers other religions as part of "God's own plan for humankind,"[225] and should not be regarded as merely a representation of "a human quest for the divine."[226] This is because God's self-revelation is an act of God's love for humankind. He posits that there are multi-dimensions but one single plan of God for humanity and that, "it belongs to the nature of the overflowing communication of the triune God to humankind to prolong outside the divine life the plural communication intrinsic to that life itself." Invariably, it is not incidental that God spoke in many diverse ways before speaking through his Son (Heb 1:11). As such, the incarnation or the Christ-event does not supersede or obsolete "the universal presence and action of the Word and the Spirit."[227]

In addition, Dupuis stresses the "constitutive uniqueness and universality" of Jesus Christ, despite the diverse universal self-manifestation of God. By this, he means that "the person

---

[224] Cf. Edward schillebeeckx, *Church: The Human Story of God* (London: SCM Press, 1990), 167.

[225] Dupuis, *Towards Christian Theology of Religious Pluralism*, 11.

[226] Ibid., 387.

[227] Ibid.

and the Christ-event 'constitute' salvation for the whole of humankind." Simply put, it means that through the paschal mystery of Christ, people despite their historical situation are granted open access to God. Dupuis further states: "The humanity of Jesus Christ, God's Son made flesh, is the sacrament of God's universal will to save. Such uniqueness must not be construed as absolute. What is absolute is God's saving will."[228]   He argues that it is God's saving will that grant salvation and not religions. Dupuis teaches that because the Christ-event is located within history, despite its significance, it is particular in time but universal in meaning. It is "singularly unique," however, "it relates to all other divine manifestations to humankind in one history of salvation – that is relational."[229]   In analyzing what Dupuis means by 'relational' role of Jesus with other religions, Knitter explains that the fullness of God's revelation to humanity is focused in Jesus; "but to increase the depth of the picture, Christians have to relate what they have in Jesus to what the Spirit is doing in other religions. Indeed, Christians don't really know the fulness of God's message in Christ unless they talk with others."[230]

For Dupuis, the universal action of the Word and the Spirit helps to uncover and enliven "other saving figures and traditions, truth and grace not brought out with the same vigor and clarity in God's revelation in Jesus Christ." Dupuis avers that grace and truth found in other religions are not to be viewed as "seeds" or "stepping-stones" to be nurtured or superseded by Christian revelation, but they rather "represent additional and autonomous benefits. More divine truth and grace are found operative in the entire history of God's

---

[228] Ibid.

[229] Ibid., 388.

[230] Knitter, *Introducing Theologies of Religions*, 92.

dealings with humankind than are available simply in Christian tradition."[231]

3.3.3. Ways of Salvation

The universal salvation of God made particular in Jesus according to Dupuis implies that Christ's paschal mystery constitutes according to God's design, a universal significance for the whole of humankind. However, in what way does one account for how divine salvation in Jesus reaches out to the members of other religions? Dupuis argues: "their own religious practice is the reality that gives expression of the experience of God and of the mystery of Christ." He insists that for Christians to refuse this notion will be to commit the error of "separation of personal subjective religious life and objective religious tradition – made up of words, rites and sacraments – in which the former is expressed."[232] Reflecting on the possibility of mediation in other religions, Dupuis teaches: "Christ, it will be suggested, is, among different saving figures in whom God is hiddenly present and operative, the one 'human face' in whom God, while remaining unseen, is fully disclosed and revealed."[233] This conviction led Dupuis to deduce:

> It seems legitimate, in concluding, to point to a convergence between the religious traditions and the mystery of Jesus Christ, as representing various, though not equal, paths along which, through history, God has sought and continues to seek human beings in his Word and his Spirit.[234]

---

[231] Ibid., 388.

[232] Ibid., 319.

[233] Ibid., 283.

[234] Ibid., 328.

Dupuis' inclusive Christology or inclusive pluralism is an effort to propound a Christian theology of religion that will be more open in dialogue with other religions. It hopes to combine the uniqueness and universality of the Christ-event to avoid two extremes of exclusivism and pluralism. For him, without "universality, uniqueness is exclusive, without uniqueness, universality would lead us down the pluralist path."[235]

Dupuis' works received critical clarifications from the Congregation for the Doctrine of Faith (CDF), which is contained in the notification given to Dupuis relating to his book, *Towards a Christian Theology of Religious Pluralism*.[236]Morali notes that the Congregation recognized Dupuis' intellectual honesty in reflecting on such issues, and further describes the intent of the Notification, thus:

> The notification, which does not intend to express 'a judgment on the author's subjective thought,' is aimed above all at enunciating the doctrine of the

---

[235] Jacques Dupuis, *Jesus Christ at the Encounter of World Religions* (Maryknoll, N.Y.: Orbis Books, 1991),192.

[236] The Congregation for the Doctrine of Faith has the delegated authority from the pope to exercise vigilance over the teaching of Catholic doctrines. The congregation has the onus of setting forth the official positions of the church, and to condemn opinions that are judged to be contrary to the Catholic faith. Cf. Francis A. Sullivan, "Introduction and Ecclesiological Issues," *Sic et Non: Encountering Dominus Iesus,* ed., Stephen J. Pope and Charles Hefling (MaryKnoll, NY: Orbis Books, 2002), 47-56.

[236] Congregation for the Doctrine of Faith: *Dominus Iesus: On the Unicity and Salvific Universality of Jesus Christ and the Church,* http://www.vatican.va/roman_curia/congregations/cfaith/documents/rc_con _cfaith_doc_20000806_dominus-iesus_en.html (accessed May 21, 2017), no. 3. Subsequent quotations from this document will be taken from this site, and will be cited as Dominus Iesus.

Church and at the same time confuting erroneous interpretations to which these theses expounded in the book might lend themselves, independently of the author's good intentions.[237]

The congregation accuses it of containing, "notable ambiguities and difficulties on important doctrinal points, which could lead a reader to erroneous or harmful opinions."[238] Among other clarifications on "the sole and universal salvific mediation of Jesus Christ," the congregation deems it erroneous "to posit a separation between the Word and Jesus, or between the Word's salvific activity and that of Jesus," but also to maintain that "there is a salvific activity of the Word as such in his divinity, independent of the humanity of the Incarnate Word." As well, on the uniqueness and definiteness of revelation in Jesus Christ, the Congregation also deems it erroneous to hold that such elements of truth and goodness, or some of them, as found in other religions, "do not derive ultimately from the source-mediation of Jesus Christ." The document further states:

> It is therefore legitimate to maintain that the Holy Spirit accomplishes salvation in non-Christians also through those elements of truth and goodness present in the various religions; however, to hold

---

[237] Ilaria Morali, "Salvation, Religions, and Dialogue in the Roman Magisterium: From Pius IX to Vatican II and Postconcilliar Popes," in *Catholic Engagement with World Religions: A Comprehensive Study*, eds., Karl J.Becker and Ilaria Morali (Maryknoll, NY: Orbis Books, 2010), 138.

[238] Congregation for the Doctrine of Faith, "Notification on the book Towards a Christian Theology of Religious Pluralism by Fr. Jacques Dupuis," http://www.vatican.va/roman_curia/congregations/cfaith/documents/rc_con _cfaith_doc_20010124_dupuis_en.html (accessed May 21, 2017).

that these religions, considered as such, are ways of salvation, has no foundation in Catholic theology, also because they contain omissions, insufficiencies and errors-regarding fundamental truths about God, man and the world.[239]

Prior to the issuance of the notification to Dupuis, the Congregation had issued a Declaration: *Dominus Iesus*.[240] According to the declaration, the aim was to remind both theologians and all the faithful of Catholic Church of "certain indispensable elements of Christian faith that will help theological reflection in developing solutions consistent with the Roman Catholic faith."[241] This declaration addresses all the issues raised on the notification to Dupuis. However, the declaration has provoked numerous criticisms both within and outside of the Roman Catholic Church, as drawing back all the efforts made since the Vatican II Council in the area of interreligious and ecumenical dialogue.[242]

Despite the controversies and criticisms against Dupuis' theology of religions, there have been some faithful disciples and ardent defenders of Dupuis' approach. For example,

---

[239] Ibid.

[240] Dominus Iesus, no. 3.

[241] Ibid.

[242] For further reading on the controversies of Dominus Iesus, see; Francis A. Sullivan, "Introduction and Ecclesiological Issues," in *Sic et Non: Encountering Dominus Iesus,* ed., Stephen J. Pope and Charles Hefling (Maryknoll, NY: Orbis Books, 2002),47-56. Jacque Dupuis, "The Declaration Dominus Jesus and My Perspective on It,"in *Jacque Dupuis Faces the Inquisition,* ed., William Burrows (Eugene, Oregon: Pickwick Publications, 2012), 26-73.

Dupuis' inclusive Christology has been described by Ambrose Ih-Ren Mong as an "attempt to interpret the church's teaching on non-Christian religions in the light of Vatican II's call for more openness and dialogue."[243] Similarly Gerald O'Collins, applauds Dupuis' work because it "converged with the official teachings and activities of John Paul II, and provided it with a massive theological underpinning."[244]

Next, I will evaluate Dupuis' 'inclusive pluralism' and D'Costa's 'exclusive particularism' as a way of ascertaining their viability in the context of dialogue with other religions.

3.4. Evaluation of Modern Inclusivism and Interreligious Dialogue

Our analysis of the theologies of D'Costa and Dupuis reveal notable areas of divergence in their approaches. For example, D'Costa maintains a stricter Christology, which insists that the truth and goodness revealed in the religions find fulfilment in Christ. He argues that whatever the spirit reveals in the religions cannot contradict what it already revealed in Christ. Hence, Jesus has a normative role in human salvation. Even though Dupuis acknowledges the unique role of the incarnate Word in history, argues that it has its own innate limitation, which will be overcome only at the eschaton. The

---

[243] Ambrose Ih-Ren Mong, *Dialogue Derailed: Joseph Ratzinger's War against Pluralist Theology* (Eugene, OR: Pickwick Publications, 2015), 224.
[244] Gerald O'Collins, "Jacques Dupuis Contributions to Interreligious Dialogue," *Theological Studies* 64, (2003), 397.

mystery of God's revelation is not exhausted in the revelation of the incarnate Word in history. It implies that the Spirit can assume a distinct role in the religions in mediating through their tradition. The truth revealed by the Spirit among religions is not to be regarded as rays of light but added truth of God's self-revelation. He considers the role of Jesus as unique, constitutive, and relational to other manifestations of God's self-revelation to humankind.

While D'Costa does not assigning salvific status to other religions, he acknowledges elements of truth in them. Dupuis believes that other religions are according to God's plans sources of salvation for their members. It means that Christ saves members of other religions in and through their own religions and traditions. For Dupuis, Jesus role in salvation is unique but neither absolute nor relative. It is 'constitutive' and 'relational.'[245]

Their divergencies aside, as inclusivists, D'Costa and Dupuis share some commonalities. First, both thinkers embraced Trinitarian theology as a viable theological ground for Christian inclusive theology of religions. Secondly, their Christology assigns Jesus a very unique role in the mystery of salvation. Jesus Christ is God, the second person of the Trinity,

---

[245]By 'constitutive savior" Mong explains that it means, "for Christians, the paschal mystery has a universal significance; it is the 'privileged channel' through which God saves his people." And by 'relational savior,' Mong explains that it means, "there is a reciprocal relationship between the way of Jesus Christ and those of other religious tradition. It implies that God saves members of other religions through their religion, and that there is religious pluralism in fact as well as in principle. Mong, *Dialogue Derailed,* 216.

but not considered as the whole of God. Thirdly, they recognize that the Holy Spirit is active in the religions of the world, revealing goodness and truth. Finally, they agree that there is possibility of salvation for the religions of the world through the special event of the paschal mystery of Christ and by the actions of the Holy Spirit.

Critics accuse the inclusivist position of being "no more than exclusivism with a happy face. Other traditions are seen at best as satellites or derivatives of the one true way."[246] They argue that when truth and goodness revealed in other religious traditions are at best seen as rays of truth that will be brought to the true light through evangelization and conversion to Christianity, such dialogue becomes a form of proselytism. Similarly, Race criticizes Christian inclusivism as an "unjustified theological imperialism" for making *a priori* claim to "the fullness of expression of religious truth and value, without recourse to the empirical data of the other religions themselves."[247] This view is shared by Mong who argues that inclusivist approach "tends to reduce other religions to vassals of Christianity, "something less than they themselves claim to be."[248] Indeed, when Christians consider the good values in other religions as deficient of salvation, solely fulfilled in Christianity, it assumes an imperialist outlook.

---

[246] Minix, *Contemporary Inclusivism*, 83.

[247] Race, Christians and Religious Pluralism, 68.

[248] Mong, Dialogue Derailed, 38. John Hick, "The Theological Challenge of Religious Pluralism," in *Christianity and Other Religions*, eds., John Hick and Brian Hebblethwaite (Oxford: Oneworld Publications, 1981), 160-168.

Acknowledging the criticisms against *apriori* interpretative approach of inclusivist on other religions, Cheetham observes:

> Inclusivism [...] supplies an unwarranted hermeneutical layer that precludes the other religion's self-interpretation [...] it is a patronizing approach that assumes at the outset what is really going on in another religion. Worst still, it may even be deficient when it comes to engendering a proper attitude towards the other. Thus, the inclusivistic 'owning' of the other's discourse is essentially a refusal to learn about other religions on their own terms.[249]

After acknowledging this tendency in interreligious dialogue, Cheetham proposes that "dialogue must become an essential activity where authentic voices can be heard and conversations between faiths develop." In this way, dialogue is seen no longer as patronizing, but an exercise in charity. It becomes an "open gesture that seeks out the best in the other (and the other's wellbeing) within one's own narrative."[250]

It is this approach of dialogue that is proposed by Dupuis and D'Costa in their forms of inclusivism. Inclusivism that embraces two important dispositions necessary for dialogical engagements: commitment to one's own religious confession and openness to acknowledging the good in the other religions. Commitment to one's religion does not exclude the others, instead it recognizes that the other person has something to bring to the table of dialogue. According to John Paul II,

---

[249]David Cheetham, "Inclusivisms: Honouring Faithfulness and Openness," 77.

[250] Ibid., 78.

"dialogue without foundations would be destined to degenerate into empty wordiness."[251] This balanced disposition is necessary for dialogue as Cornille expresses; "if dialogue is to be possible, it must find deepest reasons and motivations within the self-understanding of religious traditions themselves." She maintains that it is only under this condition will dialogue be considered an "internal necessity and not an external obligation."[252] In affirmation, Thomas Reynolds stresses that an effective dialogue is to be "rooted variously in affirmation central to particular faith communities."[253] Above all, this approach ensures proper grounding in ones' religious tradition and equips people to make significant contributions at the dialogue table instead of approaching dialogue baselessly.

For Dupuis, "sincerity in dialogue specifically requires that the various partners enter it and commit themselves to it in the integrity of their faith." Effective dialogue does not admit any syncretism or other "quest for a common ground." It acknowledges differences "where they exist and face them patiently and respectfully." In the same vein, dialogue forbids toning down deep convictions on either side, it "seeks understanding in difference, in a sincere esteem for convictions other than one's own." Dupuis surmises that openness and commitment are not mutually exclusive but must be combined for effective dialogue. In further defense of Christian inclusivist position, Dupuis states: "Christian identity, as it has

---

[251]Pope John Paul II, "Statement at the Recitation of the Angelus 1 October 2000." See *Sic et Non: Encountering Dominus Iesus*, eds., Stephen J. Pope and Charles Hefling, (Maryknoll, NY: Orbis Books, 2002), 34.

[252] Cornille, *The Im-possibility of Dialogue*, 8.

[253] Thomas Reynolds, "Theology and Religious Others: The Unity of Love of God and Neighbor and Interreligious Hermeneutics," *Science et Espirit* 68, no.2-3 (2016), 257.

been understood through the centuries, is linked to faith in the "fullness" of divine revelation in Jesus Christ, but they must be understood without either reductionism or exclusivism."[254]

The recognition and acknowledgement of elements of truth and goodness in other religions will enable Christians and Muslims enrich each other through the spiritual riches embedded in other religion. It informs D'Costa's approach to dialogue as a two-way fulfilment process. Since the Spirit pervades all creation and is active in the world religions, "then the world religions are vital to Christian faithfulness," because the Spirit may surprise us from what it reveals through them.[255] In the same vein, Dupuis insists on the need for mutual acceptance of differences" and "even contradictions," together with the respect of free decision made with conscience on the part of the interlocutor.[256]

The affirmation of elements of truth and goodness in other religious traditions opens vistas of trust and greater commitment in dialogical engagements. It opens the hearts of people in the dialogical encounter to work together in the areas of human liberation. In relation to this, D'Costa maintains that "the normativity of Christ involves a normativity of crucified self-giving love."[257] According to him, this is made concrete in the "love of neighbor," because it is "co-essential with the love of God." It is when, through both personal adversities and the eagerness to see "the real needs of our neighbors, especially in their marginalization, suffering, poverty and vulnerability" that Christians model their lives on that of Christ. Such

---

[254] Dupuis, *Christianity and the Religions*, 230.
[255] D'Costa, *Christian Uniqueness*, 23.
[256] Dupuis, *Towards a Christian Theology of Religions*, 367.
[257] D'Costa, Christian Uniqueness Reconsidered, 20.

engagements with people from other faith traditions, will create trust and openness in dialogue.[258]

Dupuis emphasizes the need and "the call to unite the praxis of human liberation and interreligious dialogue into one concern." He reflects on the theology of Aloysius Pieris, which locates poverty and multiplicity of religions as common denominators in Asia and other developing countries, and points out the urgency for the expansion of "the existing boundaries of orthodoxy" in order to enter into the "liberative streams of other religions and cultures."[259] Dupuis argues that for dialogue to be effective there should be an expansion of dialogue from theoretical discourse to an imperative of what Hans Kung describes as "global ethic," and Knitter describes as "globally responsible" dialogue. It is a dialogue among religions that tackles social injustice and ecological abuse as our common human problems.[260] It means that inclusivism embraces the involvement with other religions in works of social justice. One does not necessarily need to be a pluralist to engage in this form of dialogical commitment.

D'Costa and Dupuis through their interpretation of Christian Trinitarian Theology have proposed effective ways of engaging in dialogue with other religions. As I noted above, the criticism of inclusive typology is its seemingly imperialist approach; the categories of Christian faith, like the Trinitarian theology, are employed as the starting point for dialogue

---

[258] Ibid.

[259] Cf. Aloysius Pieris, "The Place of Non-Christian Religions and Culture in the Evolution of the Third World Theology," *Irruption of the Third World: Challenge to Theology*, ed. V. Fabella and S. Torres(Maryknoll, NY: Orbis Books, 1983), 113-114.

[260] Dupuis, *Towards a Christian Theology of Religious Pluralism,* 377.

towards the assimilation of other religious categories into Christian religion. Such "assimilation", however, despite perils, need not be necessarily imperialistic, but rather, more like understanding another from within the categories of what is perceived as true vis-à-vis one's own perspective, and may thus be natural part of the way religious traditions engage one another. Equally, then, non-Christian religions like Islam may be seen to have similar default position, by beginning with the categories of their own religious self-understanding in dialogue with Christianity.

3.5.   Islam and Inclusivism

In this section, I will briefly explore the teachings of two Muslim theologians from two different Islamic traditions to accentuate the potentials in other inclusivist viewpoints other than Christianity. The aim is to highlight how encounters between two different traditions with inclusivist approaches may result in fruitful dialogue in the Nigerian context.

3.6. Amir Hussain: From Tolerance to Dialogue

Amir Hussain is a Sunni Muslim and a Professor of Theological Studies at Loyola Marymount University in Los Angeles, he was born in Pakistan before moving to Canada with his family. He has written widely on interfaith dialogue. His book entitled, *Oil and Water*, is an introduction to Islam in the context of dialogue with Christianity. It is a post 9-11 apologetics on the true faith of Islam. In his writing, he has highlighted areas of inclusive engagement with Christianity from the Qur'an and Islamic history. The following section discusses some of his teachings to identify inclusivist elements from Islam to bolster fruitful dialogue with Christianity.

3.6.1. The People of the Book (ahk al-kitab)

The Qur'an refers to Jews, Christians and Zoroastrians as "people of the book." According to Hussain, the Qur'an encourages cordial relations and inter-marriage between them:

> Today all good things have been made lawful for you. The food of the people of the book is lawful for you as your food is lawful for them. So are chaste, believing, women as well as chaste women of the people who are given the scriptures before you, as long as you have given them their bride-gifts and married them, not taken them as lovers or secret mistresses (Qur'an 5:5).

Hussain avers that this makes relationship between Christians and Muslim religiously affirmative. Similarly, the Qur'an acknowledges the good deeds of righteous Christians, which will be rewarded by God:

> There are some among the people of the book who are upright, who recite God's revelations during the night, who bow down in worship, who believe in God and the Last Day, who order what is right and forbid what is wrong, who are quick to do good deeds. These people are among the righteous and they will not be denied [the reward] for whatever good deeds they do: God knows exactly who is conscious of him (Qur'an 3:113-115).[261]

For this reason, Hussain contends that the Qur'an "envisions a peaceful co-existence that emanates from a

---

[261] Amir Hussain, *Oil and Water: Two Faith One God* (Kelowna: CopperHouse, 2006), 185.

common revelation and God."[262] In fact, the Qur'an exhorts Muslims to eschew argument with the people of the book: "[Believers], argue only in the best way with the people of the book, except with those of them who act unjustly. Say, we believe in what was revealed to us and in what was revealed to you; our God and your God is one [and the same]; we are devoted to Him" (Qur'an 29:46). What this passage implies is that Islam upholds the inclusive beliefs in the one God and living a life of justice as reward of everlasting life. Hussain believes that these grounds should form the locus for peaceful co-existence and constructive dialogue between Islam and Christianity.

3.6.2. Jesus as the Focal Point for Dialogue

According to Hussain, the regard that both Christians and Muslims have for the person of Jesus should form "another bridge towards inclusivity" in their relationship.[263] This is because Jesus is an important prophet for the Muslims, and is mentioned in 15 chapters and 93 verses of the Qur'an. He points out that even though Jesus is a Jew, he is not designated any significance in Jewish religion, however, in Islam, Jesus is acknowledged with great regard. Nonetheless, Hussain outlines some substantial differences in the understanding of the person of Jesus by Christians and Muslims. For example, although the Muslims acknowledge Jesus as Messiah and a Messenger of God, and ascribe miracles and virgin birth to him, they refute him divinity: "People of the book, do not go to excess in your religion [...] the messiah, Jesus, Son of Mary, was nothing more than a messenger of God, His word directed to Mary, and

---

[262] Ibid.
[263] Ibid., 191.

a spirit from Him" (Qur'an 4: 171). Hussain argues that like the Jews, the Muslims do not believe in original sin nor rely on someone to die as atonement for their sins. The Muslims do not believe that Jesus was sacrificed for their sin, and even denies that he died on the cross.[264]

Despite the differences in belief patterning to the person of Jesus Christ, Hussain contends that "the esteem in which both faith communities hold Jesus should keep them in dialogue."[265] Regardless of the differences, Hussain proposes unrelenting engagement on interfaith dialogue between the two religions. Hussain writes: "Our differences and ensuing disputes are not to be feared, denied or eradicated. God teaches us through our differences. It is through dialogue that we learn about ourselves, about others and in so doing, perhaps about God."[266] The implication is that dialogue approached through inclusivist categories in Islamic and Christian traditions will promote collaborative and fruitful dialogical encounters.

3.7. Reza Shah-Kazemi: The Qur'an and Inclusivism

Reza Shah-kazemi is an Ismaili Shia Muslim scholar, and the founding editor of the *Islamic World Report*. Shah-Kazemi is currently a Research Associate at the Institute of Ismaili Studies with the Department of Academic Research and Publications. He has published severally on Islam and interreligious dialogue. In this section, I will examine some of his reflections on the Qur'an relating to interreligious dialogue.

---

[264] Amir Hussain, "From Tolerance to Dialogue: A Muslim Perspective on Interfaith Dialogue with Christians," *Asian Christian Review*2 no.2&3 *(2008)*, 96.

[265] Ibid.

[266] Hussain, *Oil and Water,* 197.

3.7.1. The Qur'an and the Spirit of Tolerance

In our present socio-religious setting, Shah-Kazemi, identifies two causes for the negative perception of Islam as a religion devoid of tolerance. The first is engendered by islamophobia among non-Muslims. The second is caused by Muslim fanatics who engage in acts that are not congenial with people of other religious faith. Shah-Kazemi believes that it is necessary to correct the erroneous perception of Islam using the interpretation of the Qur'an and the tolerant spirit of Islam. He recommends that "any contemporary effort to review or revive the integral tradition of tolerance in Islam should first and foremost be on the verse of the Qur'an."[267] Shah-Kazemi's interpretation of Qur'an 5:48, portrays that God wills the diversity of religions:

> We have assigned a law and a path to each of you. If God had so willed, He would have made you one community, but He wanted to test you through that which He has given you, so race to do good: you will all return to God and He will make clear to you the matters you differed about. So [prophet] judge between them according to what God has sent down. Do not follow their whims, and take good care that they do not tempt you always from any of what God has sent down to you.

This Qur'anic passage obliges believers to the tolerance of other faiths since God wills them to exist.

---

[267] Reza Shah-Kazemi, *The Spirit of Tolerance in Islam* (London:I.B. Tauris Publishers, 2012), 75.

Although this passage affirms the divine root of other religion, it seems to strike a tone of supersession: "Judge between them according to what has been sent down. Do not follow their whims, and take good care that they do not tempt you always from any of what God has sent down to you" (Qur'an 5:49). Shah-Kazemi referred to Tim Winter who described it as a "non-categoric supersession." It is supersession "according to which the religions deemed to have been superseded by Islam retain in different degree, their salvific efficacy on account of revelation at the source of their tradition."[268] This interpretation aligns closely to the Vatican II description of other religions as containing the "rays of light, which enlightens all people." It is also in consonance with the theologies of D'Costa as discussed in chapter two above. In this case, Islam is laying the same claim of fullness of revelation. However, this does not detract from the fact that, the divine root of religions as revelled by the Qur'an lays an ethical obligation of tolerance on Muslims. Shah Kazemi affirms:

> Qur'an is God's final, and most complete revelation to mankind. Part of this completeness entails, precisely its unique embrace of all revelations, its unique perspective on the plurality of the religious phenomenon, and thus its concomitant emphasis on tolerance of, and respect for, believers in communities founded by authentic revelation of God.[269]

---

[268] Cf. Shah-Kazemi, *The Spirit of Tolerance*, 88.
[269] Ibid.

Shah-kazemi alludes to Ibn al-Arabi's view of Naskh, who used the phenomenon of the sun and the stars to illustrate this idea. According to this view, other religions are like lights of the stars, while the religion of Muhammad is like the sun. When the sun appears, the lights of the stars are either hidden under or united to the light of the sun, but they are neither abrogated nor destroyed. Thus, Shah-Kazemi concludes that "from the inclusive point of view, Islam encompasses all revelations, which can thus be seen as so many different facets of the same principle of submission."[270]

Further analyzing the verse, Shah-Kazemi interprets the passage: "He wanted to test you through that which He has given you, so race to do good" (Qur'an 5:48), as intended by God in order to "stimulate a healthy competition or mutual enrichment in the domain of good work." For the good ordering of society, good work is required, but is also necessary for the attainment of life hereafter. According to the Qur'an; "For the [Muslim] believers, the Jews, Sabians, and Christians – those who believe in God and the Last Day and do good deeds – there is no fear: they will not grieve" (Qur'an 5:69). Shah-Kazemi explains that the competition in good deeds as enjoined by the Qur'an has nothing to do with superiority of ones' religion. On the contrary, it refers to the overcoming of personal ego to render total submission to God in the service of others. Therefore, virtue or good work is closely related to human participation in the two great attributes or qualities of God among the Muslims: "compassionate and merciful."[271] According to Shah-Kazemi:

---

[270] Ibid.

[271] The two names or attributes of God: *al-Rahman* and *al-Rahim*, compassion and mercy are given in the formula by which every significant act in Islam is consecrated, and with which almost all the chapters of the

Whenever God is described in terms of compassion and peace and love, it always implies that the soul is being called upon to assimilate these qualities: Those names and qualities that characterize God must also characterize man-mutatis mutandis; what is true of God in absolute mode must be true of man in relative mode.[272]

The implication is that Islamic faith obliges Muslims to live out mercy and compassion in their relationship with all peoples. Invariably, this enables the forging of a dialogical relationship between Muslims and people of some other faiths, especially Christians.

Furthermore, even though, love *per se,* is not used in the Qur'an as one of the ninety-nine names of *Allah*, God is, however, described as "The Loving," *al-Wadud*, thus implying the quality of love (hubb). Of course, there are such verses as: "And he is the forgiving, the loving" (Qur'an 85:14), and "Ask forgiveness of your lord, then turn to him repentant. Truly my Lord is merciful, loving" (11:90). However, Shah- Kazemi explains:

> The Muslim does not view God's love through the prism of divine name *al-Wadud,* nor still less through the spectacles of theology; rather, the love of God is perceived and received as an all-embracing quality of creative being, and not simply conceived as an anthropomorphic emotion.[273]

Qur'an begin. This formula is known as the *basmala.* Reza Shah-Kazemi, *My Mercy Encompasses All: The Koran's Teachings on Compassion, Peace and Love* (Shoemakers Hoard: Emeryville, CA, 2007), 11.

[272]Ibid.

[273] Reza Shah-Kazemi, "God, 'The Loving,'" in *A Common Word:*

Regarding the qur'anic basis for the assertion that God is inherently and overwhelming loving, he argues that one must focus on the two names for mercy: *al-Rahman* and *al- Rahim*. He elucidates that "God's *rahma* refers not only to mercy or compassion but also, and fundamentally to the infinite love and overflowing beatitude of ultimate reality."[274]

The quality of *rahma* is also exemplified in the life of the prophet, which as the Qur'an states: "We sent you not [O prophet] save as a mercy for all the world" (Qur'an 39:53). The prophet is named *al-habib*, the beloved, or *habibu'Llah*, the beloved of God. The prophet says: If you love God, follow me. God will love you" (3:31). Interpreting this verse Shah-Kazemi writes:

Following means ensuring that mercy, love and gentleness prevail within our souls, this being our way of mirroring the predominance of the same qualities within Ultimate Reality. It follows that entering into the mould of prophetic love is to enter into the realm of the Real, and herein lies the fundamental aim not just prophet's mission, but of all prophecy, in all ages and all places.[275]

The love of God expressed in the Qur'an as epitomized in the life of Prophet Muhammed, forms the inclusive grounds for dialogical relationship between Christian and Muslims.[276]

Muslim and Christians on Loving God and Neighbor, eds., M. Volf, G. Muhammad and M. Yarrington (Grand Rapids, MI: William B. Eerdmans Publishing Company, 2010), 101.

[274] Ibid., 109.

[275] Ibid., 108.

[276] Shah-Kazemi, *The Spirit of Tolerance in Islam*, 128.

3.8. Evaluation of Inclusivism in Islam

Hussain and Shah-Kazemi in their theologies and interpretations of the Qur'an laid claims to the inherent openness and tolerance of Islam in relation to other religions. However, there are several exclusivist passages in the Qur'an. For example: "You who believe, do not take the Jews and the Christians as allies; they are allies only to each other. Anyone who takes them as an ally becomes one of them – God does not guide such wrongdoers" (Qur'an 5:51). In another passage, the Qur'an condemns Christian fundamental doctrine of the Trinity and of the incarnation:

> Those people who say that God is the third of three are defying [the truth]: there is only one God. If they do not stop what they are saying a painful punishment will afflict those of them who persist. The Messiah, son of Mary, was only a messenger; other messengers had come and gone before him…say, people of the book, do not overstep the bounds of truth in your religion and do not follow the whims of those who went astray before you – they led many others astray and themselves continue to stray from the path" (5:73-77).

Shah-Kazemi acknowledges such passages, however, he defensively argues: "If Muslims faith were based on such verses alone, the result would be diatribe than dialogue."[277] So, it is imperative from such justification to find a broader context for understanding the relation of Islam to other religions.

---

[277] Reza Shah-Kazemi, *The Other in the Light of the One: The Universality of the Qur'an and Interfaith Dialogue* (Cambridge: Islamic Text Society, 2006), 213.

Conversely, the Qur'an consists of several other inclusive verses in relation to the people of the book. Nevertheless, these may not be a satisfactory response to Muslims who hold tenaciously to these exclusive verses. Shah-kazemi proposes:

> One way of ensuring that these theological differences do not result in hostility is to acknowledge them openly, and not pretend that they are negligible; for when the distinctive features of deeply held doctrines are dismissed as negligible, that is when defensive reflexes set in.[278]

This proposal resonates with Dupuis' argument in defence of inclusivism in Christianity, where he avers that dialogue acknowledges differences where they exist and faces them patiently. Dupuis insists that dialogue forbids devaluation of deep convictions on either side but rather seeks understanding.[279] Nonetheless, the following verses from the Qur'an invoke the sense of violence against non-Muslims: "When the [four] forbidden months are over, wherever you encounter the idolaters, kill them, seize them, besiege them, wait for them at every lookout post" (Qur'an 9:5). Fundamentalist Muslims who look for reasons to fight non-Muslims and Islamophobes, who depict Islam as a religion of violence widely quote this verse to justify their inhuman actions. Hussain argues that the passage has a particular historic context and ought not to be applied to our present context. He clarifies:

> [I]t is a violence that is contextualized, meaning it occurs in the context of warfare between Muslims and polytheists. Finally, it is a violence that is

---

[278] Ibid., 230.

[279] Dupuis, *Christianity and the Religions*, 230.

tempered as following verse indicates: "fight in the cause of God those who fight you but do not transgress limits. Surely God does not love transgressors" (2:190).[280]

Relating this to the usage of the word jihad, which is wrongly interpreted as holy war, Hussain elucidates that the word comes from the verb *jahada,* meaning "to strive or struggle in the path of God." The noun is *mujahid,* referring to "the same struggle."[281] According to Hussain, the Muslim tradition distinguishes from inner *jihad* and outer jihad. The inner *jihad* is the inner struggle of a person to become a better Muslim exemplified in the lives of mystics, and cuts across every religion. It patterns to people's attempt "to temper inclinations towards evil with an ongoing commitment to righteousness."[282] Outer jihad relates to peoples' effort to make their society reflective of the principles of submission to God. This involves works of liberation and social justice. Going by this interpretation, instead of connoting the idea of division and strife jihad should actually form an inclusive principle for dialogue between Islam and Christianity.

It is pertinent to note that just as it is with Christianity, there are plenty of Islamic authors that embrace an exclusivist approach, and find ample materials in the scriptures to support claims against other traditions. Similarly, several avenues exist for cultivating inclusivist understanding and promotion of interreligious dialogue between Christianity and Islam. Christianity and Islam teach the importance of virtuous living and love. The open letter to Christian leaders all over the

---

[280] Hussain, *Oil and Water*, 125.

[281] Ibid., 117

[282] Ibid.

world, written by 138 Muslim leaders at the end of Ramadan in 2007 entitled, *A Common Word Between Us and You*, rightly considers the love of God and love of neighbor as a common ground for engagement in dialogue between the two religions. The document exhorts:

> It is part of the very foundational principles of both faiths: love of the One God, and love of the neighbour. These principles are found over and over again in the sacred texts of Islam and Christianity. The Unity of God, the necessity of love for Him, and the necessity of love of the neighbour is thus the common ground between Islam and Christianity.[283]

When Christians and Muslim embrace the correlating commands of love of God and love of neighbor, the person of the other religion is seen as ones' neighbors. In such manner, peaceful co-existence and fruitful dialogue become feasible. Therefore, there is the need to consider this fundamental element of both Islam and Christianity religions as bases for dialogical engagements.

3.9. Conclusion

Dialogue between Christians and Muslims is a complex engagement with considerable prospects and challenges. In this chapter, I have explored through the prism of few Christian and Muslim theologians, how theological conceptions of inclusivism built from the perspective of a religious tradition

---

[283]"A Common Word Among Us and You," http://www.acommonword.com/the-acw-document/ (accessed June 11, 2017).

embodies the prerequisites for interreligious dialogue, and can promote peaceful coexistence between Christians and Muslims. Inclusivism overcomes on the one hand, the exclusive attitude that makes dialogue difficult, on the other hand, the plurality that denies the irreducible particularity of a religion, leading to relativism or other forms of exclusivism. Furthermore, it accords respect to the particularity of the religious other without trivializing the core beliefs of ones' own religion. Affirming the importance of respect to the particular of religions and its relevance in the wider dynamism of dialogical encounter, Reynolds states:

> Dialogue begins with particularity and differences. And more, dialogue assumes the maintaining of particular claims that implicate the other. The Christian affirmation of God, for instance, has a universal sweep in that God is identified as creator, sustainer and redeemer of all that is, and such an affirmation connects all humanity and history.[284]

Not only is respect of the particularity of the other faith needed in the fostering of dialogue, according to Reynolds, there is also the need to presume that the "other party's particularity is worth engaging." There is need for an orientation that does not "preclude but rather predisposes members towards dialogical openness and engaging religious others as having something to say."[285] The correlating love of God and love of neighbor are virtues that emanate from deep religious commitment in the teachings of the Qur'an and the Bible. The recognition of the religious other as neighbor who

---

[284] Reynolds, "Theology and Religious,"262.
[285] Ibid.

deserves love, stems from the convictions of Islamic faith and extends to the ideals of the Christian teachings on love of God and neighbor. Hence, love provides the openness and commitment needed in dialogue.

The orientation towards dialogical encounter between Christians and Muslims finds its strong impetus toward engaging in acts of loving relationship. As the theologies of D'Costa, Dupuis, Hussain and Shah-Kazemi have shown, love is essential in fostering peaceful relations between the two religions. Therefore, the theoretical ideals and principles of inclusivism become more productive when embodied in practical exchange and engagement in the works of love towards ones' neighbour. In the next chapter, I will explore the applicability of this dialogical praxis to the Nigerian context.

Chapter Four

The Proposition of Dialogue of Life and Action in the Nigerian Context

4.1. Introduction

This chapter builds on the foregoing discussion to explore the application of theological inclusivism as a dialogical praxis in building a lasting peaceful co-existence between Christians and Muslims in Nigeria. This will be realized through a brief contextualization of the four forms of interreligious dialogue as listed by some official ecclesiastical document.[286] These include dialogue of theological exchange, dialogue of spiritual exchange, dialogue of action and dialogue of life.

In this chapter, emphasis will be laid on dialogue of life and action or social dialogues. These two forms of dialogue correspond with inclusivist categories in both Islam and Christianity. They apply the Christian ideals of *Caritas* and Islamic ideals of *Rahma*in practical life context. This chapter contends that Christian-Muslim dialogue in Nigeria can yield much fruit, when interreligious dialogue grounded on the hermeneutics of theological inclusivism of both religions is applied in the praxis of dialogue of life and action.

4.2. Forms of Interreligious Dialogue and the Nigerian Experience

Dialogue between Christianity and other world religions is a complex engagement which implies the reciprocal interaction between people to achieve a common goal. The Pontifical Council for Interreligious Dialogue in the document, *Dialogue*

---

[286] The documents include: Dialogue and Mission, Dialogue and Proclamation, and *Redemptoris Missio.*

and Proclamation, defines interreligious dialogue as including "all positive and constructive interreligious relations with individuals and communities of other faiths which are directed at mutual understanding and enrichment, in obedience to truth and respect for freedom."[287]The complexity of this engagement has led to the classifications of different dialogical approaches. These different forms of dialogue do not exist in isolation, but they overlap when applied towards fostering peaceful co-existence among religions.

4.3 Dialogue of Theological Exchange

Dialogue of Theological Exchange occurs when theologians of different religious affiliations create a platform for discussion on major theological issues to gain better insight into shared beliefs and values. *Dialogue and Proclamation,* describes it as a process "where specialists seek to deepen their understanding of their respective religious heritages, and to appreciate each other's spiritual values."[288]While this form of dialogue has been criticized because of its theoretical approach, and suitability for educated leaders of the religions, it goes without saying that theologians and religious leaders are the moving forces within their religions. Their interpretations and teachings on interreligious dialogue are essential in leading

---

[287]Pontifical Council for Interreligious Dialogue and Congregation for the Evangelization of People, Dialogue and Proclamation: Reflection and Orientations on Interreligious Dialogue and The Proclamation of The Gospel of Jesus Christ, http://www.vatican.va/roman_curia/pontifical_councils/interelg/docu ments/rc_pc_interelg_doc_19051991_dialogue-and-proclamatio_en.html(accessed November 14, 2017), no. 9. Subsequent quotations from this document will be taken from this site, and will be cited as Dialogue and Proclamation.

[288] Ibid., no.42.

their members to a better understanding of other religions and a commitment to dialogue. For instance, the Roman Catholic Church's transition from an exclusivist posture prior to the Vatican II Council, to its present openness to world religions involved rigorous theological reflections and exchange by experts.[289] This state of openness was not attained by practical engagement alone, but through series of profound theological analyses that produced a convincing stance for the church to become more positive to world religions.

In Christian-Muslim relations, the desire to continue engaging in this form of dialogue inspired the Pontifical Council for Interreligious Dialogue and the Islamic Economic Social and Cultural Organization (ISESCO) to form a joint committee that meets annually to dialogue on issues of interest to both religions, in order to foster understanding.[290]*Dialogue and Proclamation* has however warned against the tendency of turning this form of dialogue into a luxury of academic discussion exclusive to the academia.[291]

In the Nigerian context, dialogue of theological exchange is prevalent. Christians and Muslims have formed commissions that engage in awareness, discussions, conferences, empowerment, and education of people on religious dialogue and co-operation. The Catholic Bishops' Conference of Nigeria (CBCN), which was formed in 1956,

---

[289] John M. Oesterreicher, ''Declaration on the Relationship of the Church to Non-Christian Religions, Introduction and Commentary,'' in Commentary on the Documents of Vatican II, ed. Herbert Vorgrimler, trans. William Glen-Doepel et al. (Montreal: Palm, 1968), 46 – 84.

[290] Michael L.Fitzgerald, "Christian Muslim Dialogue: A Survey of Recent Developments," (2000), www.sedos.org/english/fitzgerald.htm (accessed, July 1, 2017).

[291] Dialogue and Proclamation, no.43

created a department within the Catholic Secretariat to help organise and foster Muslim-Christian dialogue.[292] The Catholic Bishops' Conference of Nigeria (CBCN) regularly releases communiqués after their meetings and often addresses issues relating to dialogue and peaceful co-existence between the religions. For instance, the Catholic Bishops' Conference of Nigeria (CBCN) released a statement at the height of the continuous attacks in North East Nigeria by Boko Haram in 2014, which reads:

> As Nigeria tragically bleeds and burns, we Bishops are really alarmed at the scale of human, material destruction, and the disruption of village and community life with increased levels of hatred and potentials for more conflicts in the nation. While Muslims are sometimes the targets of these destructive attacks, Christians, Churches and non-Muslims in general are the principal targets for extermination, expropriation and expulsion by the Boko Haram insurgents, the perpetrators of all these destructions. We believe that we still have governments- at Federal and State- levels whose primary duty it is to preserve and protect the life of every Nigerian irrespective of tribe, religion, social class or tradition.[293]

In fact, every Catholic diocese in Nigeria established a

---

[292] Derren A. Danjuma, "Mission and Dialogue Department of the Catholic Secretariat of Nigeria,"in *Interreligious Dialogue and Sharia*, ed.,J. Salihu (Kano, Nigeria: Jalejemi Group, 2005), 17-20.

[293] Catholic Bishops' Conference of Nigeria, *While Nigeria Bleeds and Burns,* September 18, 2014, http://www.cbcn-ng.org/ (accessed June 8,2017).

Diocesan Commission for Dialogue that facilitates outreach programmes on dialogue with other faith traditions. On the ecumenical level, Christians of all denominations formed a platform in 1976 named Christian Association of Nigeria (CAN). The original intent for the formation of CAN is to provide a forum where Christian leaders could regularly meet together and take joint actions on vital matters, "especially on issues which affect the Christian Faith and the welfare of the generality of Nigerians."[294] CAN is made up of five major Christian bodies: Christian Council of Nigeria (CCN), Catholic Secretariat of Nigeria (CSN), Christian Pentecostal Fellowship of Nigeria (CPFN)/Pentecostal Fellowship of Nigeria (PFN), Organization of African Instituted Churches (OAIC), and TEAKAN and ECWA Fellowship. CAN has over the years partnered with the Islamic groups to engage in dialogue for peaceful co-existence.

The Muslims established the Nigerian Supreme Council of Islamic Affairs (NSCIA), in 1973, as a common platform for Muslims in political and religious matters. Its branches, the Jamalat-ul-Nasril Islam (JNI) and the Council of Ulama play an advisory role, engaging in mission and dialogue.[295] Christian and Muslim leaders jointly formed the Nigerian Interreligious Council (NIREC) in September 1999, with the help of the Federal Government of Nigeria. It is made up of fifty members, with each religion providing twenty-five members. The objectives of the council include two primary elements: to foster dialogue to understand the true teachings of

---

[294]Christian Association of Nigeria, *About CAN*,http://canng.org/about-can/2-about-can (accessed January 20, 2018).

[295] Deji Ayegboyin, "Religious Association and the New Political Dispensation in Nigeria,"*Journal for Studies in Interreligious Dialogue* 15, no.1 (2005), 103-106.

Christianity and Islam, and to create a permanent and sustainable channel of communication and dialogue between Christians and Muslims. These ideas are stipulated in its constitution, and it is hoped that through regular meetings, religious and peace education, discussions, conferences, seminars and workshop, they will realize their objectives.[296]

To the credit of Nigerian Interreligious Council (NIREC), it has organized numerous conferences and workshops. Worthy of note among others is the Youth Summit on Interreligious Dialogue and Peaceful Co-existence, held in Minna in January of 2009. This conference was important because youth are vulnerable and are manipulated by politicians who whip up religious sentiments to create confusion and violence. The event recorded three hundred delegates in attendance from throughout the country. The NIREC also collaborates with other organizations to provide humanitarian services to the citizens. However, the NIREC has been criticized as being peripheral and aloof when it comes to engaging the ordinary people on the street who are impacted greatly by religious conflicts. They tend to engage in more theoretical exercises and engage in making international connection rather than facing the realities at home.

4.4. Dialogue of Religious Experience

Dialogue of religious experience takes place "where persons, rooted in their own religious traditions, share their spiritual riches, for instance, with regard to prayer and contemplations, faith and ways of searching for God or the

---

[296] Constitution of the Nigeria Interreligious Council (Abuja, Nigeria: NIREC, 2001), 1-7.

absolute."[297] A good example of this would be when Pope John Paul II gathered the leaders of all major religions in Assisi in 1986 for prayer. This form of dialogue is essential in the relationship between Christians and Muslims, especially among the contemplatives. On this note, a Catholic theologian, Ovey Mohammed points out the similarities between Christian mysticism and Islamic Sufism and how they have enriched each other. According to Mohammed, this is expressed in the solitude, contemplation, asceticism, self-forgetfulness (fana) or self-transcendence or detachment through concentration on God alone, peculiar among Christian mystics and Islamic Sufis.[298] He further observes: "Jesus is an important figure in sufism," and some refer to him as "the Seal of Sanctity." This is affirmed by a famous Spanish Sufi Muhyi al-Din Ibn Arabi (1165-1240) in his celebrated Al-Futuhat al-Makkiya (The Meccan Revelations):

> The Seal of universal holiness, above which there is no other holy, is our Lord Jesus. We have met several contemplatives of the heart of Jesus... I myself have been united to him several times in my ecstasies, and by his ministry I returned to God at my conversion... He has given me name of friend and has prescribed austerity and nakedness of spirit.[299]

It means that through the practice of contemplation, the mystics transcend beyond the attachment to a particular religion, and in their unitive state with the divine they embrace everyone that aspire towards the ultimate reality.

---

[297] Dialogue and Proclamtion, no. 42.

[298] Ovey Mohammad, *Muslim-Christian Relations: Past, Present, Future* (Maryknoll, NY.: Orbis Books, 1999), 15-16.

[299] Muhyi al-Din Ibn 'Arabi, cited in W. Stoddart, Sufism (Wellingtonborough, UK: The Aquarian Press, 1982), 70.

Some notable Christian spiritual writers and contemplatives like Thomas Merton (1915-1968), Louis Massignon (1883-1962), and Ignatius Loyola (1491-1556) acknowledged the benefits and similarities of spiritual exercises in Sufism and the Christian mysticism. Hence, Mohammed observes that the study of Christian mysticism and Sufism reveal that "for a religion to be personally authentic it must involve some direct religious experience and not be merely an affirmation of propositions accepted on the basis of authority."[300] In other words, the self-transcendence achieved through union with God, which could be related to a state of pure love, elevates one above unnecessary religious bias. Effectively, the transcendental experience forms an inclusive ground between both religions to engage in worthwhile dialogue. Obviously, while this form of dialogue is effective, its demerit is that only limited number of people could attain such height because of its discipline and rigour.

In Nigeria, there have been no confirmed engagement in the interactive and contemplative form described among the Christian and Muslim contemplatives. However, a few individuals through their conducts have shown personal transcendence when it comes to religious and political matters. Worthy of mention is Mallam Aminu Kano. According to Chinua Achebe, Aminu Kano was one of the rare upright men in Nigeria politics.[301] He has been eulogized for standing against violence, both religious and ethnic. He worked for the

---

[300] Mohammed, *Muslim Christian Relations*, 22.

[301] Chinua Achebe in his last book and personal autobiography described Mallam Aminu Kano as an upright man. He describes how uncomfortable he was, although from the Muslim North, during the genocide of the Igbo tribe during the Nigerian civil war.Chinua Achebe, *There was a Country* (New York, Penguin Press, 2012), 167, 244.

poor and fought for the emancipation of women. Unlike most Nigerian politicians, at his death, he owned only a house, no foreign or local account but a few Naira under his pillow, one farm, a wife and a daughter. He is described as "a genuine political humanist who practiced what he preached."[302] Conversely, such rare qualities are lacking in present day Nigerian politicians. Some politicians make their way to churches and mosques during political campaigns, just to get the votes of the people. Nevertheless, it will be pertinent to note that Nigerians participate in festivities of both religions. Events like wedding, funeral, thanksgiving service and other socio-religious events attract folks from both religions mingling in celebration. Also, major religious celebrations like Christmas, Easter, Eid al-Fitri, and Eid al-Mualud, which are religious feasts for the two religions respectively are designated as public holidays by the government.

4.5. The Social Dialogues

The dialogue of theological exchange and religious experience are genuine and important stages in interreligious dialogue between Christians and Muslims in Nigeria. While these two forms of dialogue often overlap with the other forms of dialogue, I will propose the dialogue of life and action as the most effective dialogues in the present Nigerian context. They are referred to as social dialogues, because they engage in the day-to-day reality of peoples' social existence. Pope Francis in his Apostolic Exhortation, *Evangelii Gaudium*, has recommended social dialogueas an effective way of carrying

---

[302] Maijama'a Sule, "Remembering Mallam Aminu Kano," in *Premium Times* (June 19, 2017), http://www.premiumtimesng.com/opinion/5163-remembering_mallam_aminu_kano.html (accessed, June 20, 2017).

out mission within the context of people of other faith to ensure peaceful co-existence. He writes:

> This dialogue is in the first place a conversation about human existence or simply, as the bishops of India have put it, a matter of "being open to them, sharing their joys and sorrows." In this way we learn to accept others and their different ways of living, thinking and speaking. We can then join one another in taking up the duty of serving justice and peace, which should become a basic principle of all our exchanges. A dialogue, which seeks social peace and justice is in itself, beyond all merely practical considerations, an ethical commitment which brings about a new social situation. Efforts made in dealing with specific themes can become a process in which, by mutual listening, both parts can be enriched. These efforts, therefore, can also express love for truth.[303]

Social dialogue or dialogue of life and action are the best options for Christian-Muslim relationship in the Nigerian present situation. This is because, it overcomes the potential superfluity of theological arguments and the ineffectiveness of ritualistic approaches but touches the hearts of people and their conditions. It is the living out of a true Christian life with love and humility, which are invaluable uniting categories of both Christianity and Islam. Although, these two forms of dialogues correlate, they have their distinctive features. In the following

---

[303] Pope Francis, *Evangelii Gaudium,*,
http://w2.vatican.va/content/francesco/en/apost_exhortations/documents/pa
pa-francesco_esortazione-ap_20131124_evangelii-gaudium.html ,(accessed on December 11, 2017), no. 250.

section, I will unpack their distinctive features in the Nigerian context to highlight their effectiveness as inclusivist approaches.

4.5.1. Dialogue of Life

Dialogue of life takes place in the ordinary daily life as Christians interact and encounter the people of other faith within their communities. According to *Dialogue and Proclamation*, this form of dialogue occurs "where people strive to live in an open and neighborly spirit, sharing their joys and sorrows, their human problems and preoccupations."[304] Describing the merit of this form of dialogue Marinus Iwuchukwu states that the healthy interaction of neighbour, co-workers, friends and family members from other religions allows people to get to "know each other better without pressure, intimidation or suspicion."[305] The implication is that this form of dialogue does not require any special training, since everyone can practice, and because it flows effortlessly and spontaneously from our very humanity as we encounter others. In addition, highlighting further the importance of dialogue of life Bevan and Schroeder, note:

> Commitment to dialogue of life, however, would help people of different faiths intentionally to get to know one another as human beings, as neighbours and fellow citizens. As people begin to see one another not in the abstract but with concrete faces and personalities, many of the fears and tensions that so often exist between practitioners of different religions can be dissolved.[306]

---

[304] Dialogue Proclamation, no. 42.

[305] Iwuchukwu, *Muslim-Christian Dialogue in Postcolonial Northern Nigeria,* 176.

Urbanization, migration and other social conditions have made it impossible not to encounter different religions in societies across the globe. This spontaneous and informal encounter of people from other religions in malls, work places, movie halls, and arenas for social events within communities creates vital locus for an important interreligious engagement and dialogue. Although, it is typically an informal dialogue, it provides essential foundation for personal encounters that will ensure better understanding among peoples of different religious backgrounds. It helps to build trust and often, lead to profound long-term relationships and partnerships. Reynolds recognizing the essential nature of this dialogical approach comments:

> [T]he first step towards fostering understanding and brokering peace and reconciliation between religious differences is often made not by agreeing on shared terms before relating to each other, but by simply agreeing to be together at all. Relation is primary. And dialogue becomes the condition upon which relationships fruitfully becomes a shared task among differences.[307]

In the practice of dialogue of life, Christians are expected to live out their vocations according to the gospel's teachings on the correlation of love of God and love of neighbour. Jesus sums up the Ten Commandments in the two actions of love of God and of neighbour (Math 22:36-40). Our neighbours include those of other faith who make up the dynamism of

---

[306] Bevan and Schroeder, *Constants in Context*, A Theology of Mission for Today (Maryknoll, NY: Orbis Books, 2004), 383.

[307] Reynolds, "Theology and Religious Others," 257.

communities where Christians inhabit. According to Reynolds, our love of God is expressed profoundly in the love of the stranger. Interpreting the passage in the gospel of Matthew: "Truly, I say to you, as you did it to one of the least of these my brethren, you did it to me" (25:45), Reynolds infers that "Christians meet Jesus in showing love to the stranger." He argues that the hospitality shown to a stranger is interwoven with love for God and Jesus. This is because in welcoming a stranger, God's love comes to heart because God loves the stranger (Deut10:17-19). Analyzing the profound implication of God's love and our hospitality to a stranger in the person of the religious other, Reynolds teaches:

Indeed, the love of God breaks the hold of self-enclosure and ushers into effect a boundary-transcending momentum towards the other in a praxis of openness, a praxis that risks a relation with the other as loved by God. In such openness, the stranger is met and welcomed as one from whom hospitality is ultimately received.[308]

The key point is that in such dialogue one does feign in a condescending way to be the righteous, charitable one, but humbly receives. Indeed, the one who is open to the stranger is enriched by the presence of the stranger who epitomizes the God who loves the stranger and whom we love. Therefore, the correlating love of God and our neighbour whom we encounter in the ordinary everyday life in our communities opens up vistas of dialogical friendship, which would ensure peaceful co-existence. Consequently, love of God and love of neighbor become a theological inclusive principle that if practiced,

---

[308] Ibid., 269.

forms the backbone for enduring and peaceful interreligious relationship between Christians and Muslim.

Relating this to the Nigeria situation, Ambrose Ukaonu considers love of God and neighbor as vital theological inclusive principle for peaceful co-existence between Muslims and Christians in Nigeria. Ukonu argues:

> The love of God shows humanity its own immense dignity and, at the same time, shows each person the same dignity inside another. Thus, it invites everyone to open himself/herself to the love for the others in a chain of reciprocal rewards of religious, political, economical, social and communitarian value. This is the basis for effective inter-religious dialogue for Nigerian development.[309]

It implies that most of the social and political challenges besetting Nigeria will find practical resolution when religions lead the way through the application of inclusive theological principle of love.

Another important intrinsic element of embracing the correlating love of God and neighbour in dialogical encounter is forgiveness. The love of God invites us to the forgiveness of others, including our enemies. In Islam God is addressed as al-Ghafur (the forgiving), because it is the nature of God to forgive. According to Mohammad Hassan Khalil, it means "that the Almighty created humans to be fallible, the God of justice and mercy may choose simply to forgive His sinful servants when they repent with sincerity."[310] The Qur'an

---

[309] Ambrose Eze Ukaonu, "Developing an Islamo-Christian Theology of Love for an Effective Inter-Religious Dialogue in Nigeria," *Journal of Inculturation Theology* 13, no.2, (2012), 164.

[310] Mohammad Hassan Khall, "Divine Forgiveness in Islamic

teaches: "Say [God says], My servants who have harmed yourselves by your own excess, do not despair of God's mercy. God forgives all sins: He is truly the Most Forgiving, the Most Merciful" (Qur'an 39:53-58). God's forgiveness extends to everyone, including Christians and pagans.[311] Therefore, God's forgiveness should inspire believers to forgive one another. The Qur'an also instructs: "Those who have been graced with bounty and plenty should not swear that they will [no longer] give to kinsmen, the poor, those who migrated in God's way: let them pardon and forgive. Do you not wish that God should forgive you? God is most forgiving and merciful" (Qur'an 24:22). The Prophet Mohammad also teaches and exemplifies this virtue of forgiveness in some of the Hadiths.[312]

Similarly, from the Christian perspective, the teaching on forgiveness assumes a paramount place in imitating Christ. On the Cross, Jesus forgave his enemies and adopted a non-violent approach in response to those who killed him (Lk.23:34). He exhorts his disciples to forgive countless time (Luke 17:4). It is in forgiveness that Christian love expresses itself, in

---

Scripture and Thought", *Sin, Forgiveness, and Reconciliation: Christian and Muslim Perspectives*, eds. Lucina Mosher and David Marshall (Washington: Georgetown University Press, 2016), 84.

[311]Jonathan A. C. Brown elucidates the profound implications of divine forgiveness, and relates it with the need of the believers to forgive others without recourse to religious affiliation. Jonathan A. C. Brown," Sin, Forgiveness and Reconciliation: A Muslim Perspective,"*Sin, Forgiveness and Reconciliation: Christian and Muslim Perspectives*, eds. Lucinda Mosher and David Marshall (Washington, DC: Georgetown University Press, 2014), 13-19.

[312] According to the Hadith Sahih al-Bukhari, it reported of how the Prophet forgave Abd Allah after his transgression in Medina, and his plans to assassinate Mohammad. Mohammad Hassan Khall, "Divine Forgiveness in Islamic Scripture and Thought," 88.

selflessness and true self-giving for the other. Explaining the self-sacrificial nature of forgiveness, Karkkainen notes that "the victim undergoes suffering in two moments: first in the act of being violated against and then in the willingness to suffer in offering the gift of forgiveness."[313]

Forgiveness helps to heal wounds of the past, thereby paving the way for reconciliation and peaceful co-existence with the religious other. Put differently, Archbishop Desmond Tutu remarks: "In the act of forgiving, we are declaring our faith in the future of a relationship and in the capacity of the wrongdoer to make a new beginning on a course that will be different from the one that caused us wrong."[314] In similar vein, Akinade considers this approach as very transformative for Christian-Muslim partners in the dialogical process. According to him, "Forgiveness provides the bedrock for pursuing the issue of justice and community building for Christians and Muslims engaged in peacemaking efforts in volatile places such as Kano, Kaduna and Jos."[315] Forgiveness heals the wounds inflicted by religious conflicts and enhances lasting peace. In his "Post Apostolic Exhortation: *Africae Munus*," Pope Benedict XVI, encourages Christians and Muslim to commit to reconciliation, justice and peace, as a way of ensuring peaceful co-existence in Africa.[316]

---

[313] Veli Matti-Karkainen, "Sin, Forgiveness, and Reconciliation: A Christian Perspective," *Sin, Forgiveness and Reconciliation: Christian and Muslim Perspectives*, eds. Lucinda Mosher and David Marshall (Washinton, DC: Georgetown University Press, 2014), 8.

[314] Desmond Tutu, *No Future without Forgiveness* (New York: Image Books, 1999), 273.

[315] Akinade, *Christian Responses to Islam in Nigeria*, 137.

[316] Pope Benedict XIV, Post Synodal Apostolic Exhortation Africae Munus, http://w2.vatican.va/content/benedict-xvi/en/apost_exhortations/documents/hf_ben-xvi_exh_20111119_africae-

In the Nigerian context, the cohabitation of Christians and Muslims across the landscape of the country and their participation in the same socio-economic and political order, ordinarily makes dialogue of life a daily routine. Christians and Muslims alike in Nigeria, share the same business, educational, political space for centuries. In some cases, they inter-marry and forge long lasting political alliance. Consequently, irrespective of religion, people are encountered as *imago Dei*, - people created out of love and imbued with the love of the same God worshipped by both religions. Relating dialogue of life to the Nigerian experience, Akinade states:

> The nonnegotiable aspect of being a Christian or a Muslim in Nigeria is common life that they share together. They are inevitably drawn into the same struggles, concerns, and agitations. The dialogue of life valorizes what is already present or occurring within the Nigerian context. It is neither a prefabricated nor a contrived form of dialogue. Rather, it is a daily engagement and encounter with people's existential realities. It wrestles with the fundamental factors and circumstances that make people human.[317]

The dialogue of life has yielded much fruit of social and religious cohesion in the South-west of Nigeria, among the Yoruba ethnic group, whose religious demographic of Christians and Muslims are approximately equal. While linking such attitude of tolerance and peaceful co-existence as emanating from the appreciation of the ethical and spiritual

---

munus.html (Accessed, June 27, 2017), no. 94.

[317] Akinade, *Christian Responses to Islam in Nigeria*, 140.

commitment of the religious other among the Yorubas, Akinade observes,

> In Yorubaland, Christians and Muslims live side-by-side, celebrate their differences and do not see doctrinal cleavages as constituting a veritable barrier to interfaith encounter and relations. The result is not lazy pluralism where the particularity of each religion is obliterated for the sake of 'getting along.' I submit that one of the significant points of departure interfaith encounters on the level of civic society among the Yoruba people is the acceptance of the presence and legitimacy of other religions as symbolic of the sacred encounter.[318]

While Southwestern Nigeria has achieved great stride in both the practice and practical manifestation of the fruits of dialogue of life, evinced in the peaceful co-existence of both religions, this unfortunately could not be said of almost any other parts of northern Nigeria. Northern Nigeria continues to experience religious conflicts between Christians and Muslims.

Unfortunately, there are instances of demonstrations of true love undocumented and unreported by the media, for instance, when Muslims in the Northern part of Nigeria had stood by the side of their Christian friends, in-laws, business associates and tenants in the face of religious conflicts, even to the point of risking their lives.[319] Indeed, not all the Muslims in the North

---

[318] Akitunde E. Akinade, Introduction: Sacred Rumbling on Christian-Muslim Encounter in Nigeria, in *Fractured Spectrum:Perspective on Christian-Muslim Encounters in Nigeria*, ed. A. Akinade (New York: Peter Lang, 2013), 2-3.

[319] In a recent communal conflict in some parts of Plateau State between Christian farmer and Fulani Herdsmen, who are predominantly

are fanatics, neither do they all support the unprovoked killing and destruction of Christian churches at the slightest provocation. Indeed, some of them have spoken eloquently and courageously against such un-Islamic behaviours among their fellow Muslims. The collaboration of both Christians and Muslims towards proper praxis of the dialogue of life will go a long way in national integration and peaceful co-existence. This can be ensured through intra- religious dialogue, a recovery of the theological category of forgiveness which is rooted in divine love for all humanity, then everyone from each of the religion will consider it a religious value and duty to forgive the religious other.

4.5.2. Dialogue of Action

Unlike the dialogue of life, which happens spontaneously because of people's co-existence in an environment, dialogue of action is an organized and planed form of dialogical and practical engagement within social situation. It grows out of dialogue of life, as people get to know each other better, trust is built, and is ready to confront and tackle shared challenges in their society. This form of dialogue takes place when Christians unite with people of other faiths in collaboration for the integral development and liberation of people. Usually, Christians and people of other faith unite in collaborative action against common problems such as; unjust social, political and social structures that are inimical to the development of their society. Referring to this form of dialogue as Dialogue of Deeds, "Dialogue and Mission" (DM),

Muslims, a Muslim Imam, saved the lives of over 200 Christians by hiding them in his Mosque and in his home. Cf.
https://www.bbc.co.uk/news/world-africa-44657339

describes it as: "deeds and collaboration with others for goal of humanitarian, social, economic, or political nature which are directed towards the liberation and advancement of mankind."[320]

The Second Vatican Council, addressing the relationship between Christians and Muslims, urges all parties to let go of the past but "to work sincerely for mutual understanding and to preserve as well as to promote together for the benefit of all mankind social justice and moral welfare, as well as peace and freedom."[321] It is in engaging in the dialogue of action that Christians and Muslims form formidable forces in combating the wave of global social concerns eroding mutual moral values shared by both religions. Addressing 8000 young people in Casablanca in Morocco on August 19, 1985, Pope John Paul II stresses the need for Christians and Muslims to join in concerted effort "to witness to him [God] by word and deed in a world ever more secularized and at times even atheistic."[322]

In Nigeria, despite the positive effects of dialogue of life, which naturally happens as Christians and Muslims share the same geographic, socio-political and economic space, it has not automatically prevented Christian-Muslim conflicts. This is partly because the realities of economic hardship created by

---

[320] The Secretariat for Non-Christian, in the document, presently the Pontifical Council for Interreligious Dialogue, published in 1984 on "The Attitude of the Church the Followers of other Religions: Reflections and Orientations on Dialogue and Mission,http://www.fabriceblee.com/uploads/3/1/6/5/3165415/dialogue_an d_mission_eng.pdf (accessed, Jan. 12, 2018), no.31.

[321] Nostra Aetate, 4.

[322] Address of His Holiness John Paul II to Young Muslims inMorocco, Monday, 19 August 1985, http://w2.vatican.va/content/john-paul-ii/en/speeches/1985/august/documents/hf_jp-ii_spe_19850819_giovani-stadio-casablanca.html (accessed, Jan. 12, 2018).

corruption, the exploitation of Nigeria's natural resources by multinational companies, bad governance, tribalism, economic sabotage and many other economic and social ills, are the underlying causes of the conflicts. According to Bishop Hassan Kukah of Roman Catholic Diocese of Sokoto, the meetings of stakeholders and leaders of religions in Nigeria have observed that dialogue of action is more beneficial to the contemporary religious problem in Nigeria.[323] Pointing out the causes, Kukah states:

> It has repeatedly been emphasized that the root cause is socio-economic poverty, which is exacerbated by illiteracy and manipulation by the political elite giving rise to social inability and insecurity and thus easy referral to religious identity as a protective platform if and when necessary. The real issues and the pressing claims of the vast majority of Nigerian Muslims and Christians are not theological; hence theology must be left out of the equation.[324]

Indeed, most religious conflicts in Nigeria are caused by harsh socio-economic situation of Nigeria, although Nigeria is richly endowed with natural and human resources. When the society and government have failed the people, they become vulnerable tools in the hands of radical religious elements who project some fundamentalist ideology on their members to be used against their fellow country-men in the name of religion.

Muslims and Christians leaders should unite in prophetic dialogue by join their voices in condemning and opposing

---

[323] Hassan Kukah and Kathleen McGarvey, "Christian-Muslim Dialogue in Nigeria," 22.

[324] Ibid., 23.

corruption that has crippled the so-called giant of Africa. Every Nigerian lay claim to a religious affiliation and no religion condone injustice and corruption. The Qur'an states: Do justice, it is nearer to piety (Qur'an 5:8), and another verse states; "God loves those who act in justice" (Quran 7:29). In the Bible, echoing the words of the prophets Isaiah, Jesus announces his mission: "The Spirit of the Lord is on me, because he has anointed me to proclaim good news to the poor. He has sent me to proclaim freedom for the prisoners and recovery of sight for the blind, to set the oppressed free" (Lk 4:18, Is. 61:1). Following the admonition of the Qur'an and emulating the life of Jesus, religious leaders should assume the voice of conscience to admonish political leaders without fear or favor and hold them accountable for their stewardship to the nation.

Pope John Paul II in his Post-Synodal Exhortation, *Ecclesia in Africa*, exhorts Christians and Muslims in their commitment to dialogue "to raise their voices against unfair policies and practices, as well as against the lack of reciprocity in matters of religious freedom." [325] This kind of action will be liberating in its outcome, because if the government is compelled to fulfill its obligation to the people, by providing education and other social amenities, the spate of religious violence will be reduced. Akinade in affirmation of the prophetic mandate of religion in dialogue of action states:

> The prophetic ability of religion lies in its ability to transcend societal restrictions and limitations. It consists of moving beyond real and artificial

---

[325] John Paul II, *Ecclesia in Africa,* http://w2.vatican.va/content/john-paulii/en/apost_exhortations/documents/hf_jpii_exh_14091995_ecclesia-in-africa.html(accessed December 8,2017), no. 66.

barriers constructed by the "powers that be" to marginalize people. The stories of religious leaders such as Jesus and Mohammed, and the Buddha are surfeited with narratives of resisting the social, economic, political, and religious norms that deface the true meaning of religion and consequently lead to subjugation and domination. These religious figures did not simply conform to societal expectations and standards. Rather, they provided radical challenges to existing paradigms and gave new meaning to religious awakening.[326]

Many individuals and organizations have established platforms for the praxis of dialogue of action in Nigeria. These platforms promote peaceful coexistence and peacebuilding among religions. Worthy of mention are Pastor James Morel Wuye and Imam Ustaz Muhammad NuraynAshafa, a Pentecostal pastor and an Islamic Imam. Whereas Pastor Wuye lost one of his hands in the religious riot in Zango region in 1992, Imam Ashafa lost relatives in the same riot. After the experience, both men came together to foster unity among Christian and Muslim youths. They later established the Interfaith Mediation Centre (IFMC), which is a platform that vigorously works for peace building between the two religions.

The Muslim/Christian Youth Dialogue Forum is a branch of the IFMC that seeks to bring Christian and Muslim youths together for interreligious understanding and peacemaking. Through this forum those who have played significant roles in the past conflicts and became victims through the physical and psychological injuries they sustained, come to realize that there

---

[326] Akinade, *Christian Responses to Islam in Nigeria*, 148-149.

is a need for a better approach to conflict resolution. In this manner, these two men's engagements in a dialogue of action, have brought their living experiences, and transformed them to serve the good of the same community. The two men have been recognized and honoured as Tanenbaum's Peacemakers in Action.[327] This is a way that collaboration among religions can transform the society.

Another interfaith platform that engages in Dialogue of Actions in Nigeria is the Kuka Centre.[328] This center was established by Bishop Kuka, a leading voice in interfaith dialogue in Nigeria. The core objective of the centre is interfaith; activities that promote conversation among Nigerian faith communities, and between the leaders of these faith communities and public policy makers. The centre promotes and engages citizens actively for inclusive dialogue and advocacy.

On the national level, the Inter-Faith Activities and Partnership for Peace (IFAPP), is another organization that engages in dialogue of action. This organization is based in the Federal Capital Territory, Abuja. It is a forum jointly created by Christians and Muslims with the goal of providing a credible and trusted platform for dialogue between people of different faiths. It provides opportunity for deliberations among religious leaders on major governance and development issues confronting Nigeria, as well as suggests appropriate response for them. It helps identify strategies and means of strengthening inter-religious relations, and to work out

---

[327] Cf. Tanebuam's, https://tanenbaum.org/peacemakers-in-action-network/meet-the-peacemakers/imam-muhammad-ashafa-pastor-james-wuye/ (accessed December9,2017).

[328] For moreinformation about The Kuka Centre: http://thekukahcentre.org/about-us/ (accessed June 28, 2017).

modalities for stemming the rising tension between Christians and Muslims.[329]

The Nigerian Interreligious Council (NIREC) also engages in initiatives involving Christians and Muslims to address the scourge of malaria, HIV/AIDS and poverty. These and a host of other organizations at the regional level, engage in dialogue of action, helping in the liberation of people, providing food and shelter, fighting injustice and create jobs for Nigerian youth. The activities of these groups have in a significant way made life easier for people and reduced religious tensions as people work together against their common problems. Therefore, an inclusive interpretation of love and justice from both the Christian tradition and the Islamic tradition combined with joint effort by members of both traditions to engage in these values will bring about lasting peace in Nigeria and in the entire world.[330]

4.6. Concluding Recommendations

The different forms of dialogues practiced in Muslim-Christian relations in Nigeria are very important as they overlap in their operation and effectiveness. However, dialogue of life and action, as proposed by this work will be more effective because of its praxis in the social context of Nigeria. The pertinent reasons for choosing these dialogical forms include; first, while Nigerians may not be interested in in-depth theological discussion or experiences, they are more easily open to social interactions with people of other faiths for better social harmony and promoting the common good.[331] Secondly,

---

[329] For moreinformation about this organization http://interfaithnigeria.org/about.html (accessed, June 28, 2017).

[330] Mohammed, *Muslim-Christian Relations*, 73.

[331] Iwuchukwu, *Muslim-Christian Dialogue in Postcolonial*

dialogue of life and action addresses the real-life issues confronting Nigerians everyday. Issues such as poverty, corruption, injustice, sickness, environmental degradation, violation of human right, conflict resolution and peace building, and other social concerns. This is because dialogue of life and action "imperatively evoke the application of inclusive theological principles or the virtues of caritas, *rahma* (compassion), justice, forgiveness, peace, and the promotion of social welfare programs."[332] These virtues form the crux of both religions' moral conduct, and are therefore, better realized in praxis.

However, to lay a proper foundation for the religious and moral necessity of collaboration between Muslims and Christians in Nigeria in the praxis of caritas and *rahma*, a proper hermeneutic and understanding of theological inclusive categories in both religions is very essential. This is implied when alluding to socio-political problems as the major causes of conflicts between religions in Nigeria, Bishop Kuka and McGarvey, acknowledge the adequate interpretation theological values in the beliefs of the religions as the keys to lasting solution to their conflicts:

> However, although the immediate problems may not be theological, it is our position that the way people view their own religion and the way they are taught to view the religion of the other necessarily has implications on how they relate to the other and to life itself.[333]

Northern Nigeria, 175.

[332] Ibid., 185.

[333] Kuka and McGarvey, "Christian-Muslim Dialogue in Nigeria," 23.

In other words, while dialogue of life and action are effective in the immediate and quick fix of these challenges, they may not be the lasting remedy to the Muslim-Christian conflict in Nigeria. There remains an urgency to build a strong foundation, a true interpretation and understanding of the categories of theological inclusivism found in Islam and Christianity that will replace the exclusivist ideological posture that keep fuelling conflict between the religions. The onus rests on theologians, pastors, imams and other leading voices in these religions to engage in radical and extensive teaching and enlightenment of their followers. I contend that Muslim-Christian dialogue in Nigeria would be productive, if dialogue of action and life are practiced with firm foundation on the hermeneutics of theological inclusivism recoverable from the teachings of both religions.

General Conclusion

The goal of this book has been to interpret theological inclusivism as an invaluable foundation for effective dialogical engagement between Christians and Muslim in Nigerian, honoring faith convictions while doing so as an opening to other religious perspectives. The incessant religious conflicts in Nigeria has led to loss of numerous lives, destruction of material resources worth millions of Naira, and resultant economic hardship, insecurity and deeper polarization of the society. Therefore, this thesis argues that proper hermeneutics of inclusive categories and the enlightenment of the adherents of Islam and Christianity would form a formidable foundation for effective interreligious dialogue. However, to properly address the conflicts between these two religions in Nigeria, there is the need to identify the factors that give rise to them.

These factors are complex as the conflicts themselves. This is because some of the factors are locally related, while some are universal factors; some are remote while some are immediate. Christianity and Islam uphold some exclusivist doctrines, which when literally interpreted by fundamentalist in both religions makes dialogue impossible. For instance, Christians lay claim to a sole and definite salvation in Jesus Christ, while Muslims claim that the Qur'anic message supersedes Christianity and Judaism, these scriptural assertions create enormous challenges for effective dialogue. In addition, the intra-conflicts among the different sects and conflicting interpretations of their beliefs and differing approaches to other religions make it difficult for any of the two religions to speak with one voice. Nigerian historical formation which saw the division of the country into Muslim North and Christian South contributed immensely to the polarization of the country. Furthermore, ethnic division engendered bias, favoritism, and politicization of religion, inept and corrupt governance, which results to socio-economic hardship and contribute directly or indirectly to the challenges of peaceful co-existence and effective interreligious dialogue.

In choosing a dialogical typology that will ensure proper and effective dialogue between Christians and Muslims in the Nigerian context, there are some prerequisites that are required. For example, people have the guarantee of freedom to exercise of their religious beliefs, which is not only an inalienable human right, but also a tenet embraced by both Christianity and Islam. Another of such prerequisite is that the interlocutor in a dialogue should be approached as an equal who has something to bring to the table of dialogue. It means, acknowledging that there are values of goodness and truth in the religion of the interlocutor and that of the participants. This prevents dialogue from turning to a monologue or worst to diatribe or one party assuming a triumphalist posture. Interreligious dialogue is to be practiced with love, humility and respect. Love for God and neighbor is a basic teaching of Christianity and Islam. Love opens one's heart for the other and ensures mutual respect. Lastly, there should be commitment. Firstly, to one's religious faith. Being able to understand and embrace those values of one's religion that opens a path to inclusive engagement. Secondly, commitment to dialogue with the religious other. These prerequisites guide towards the choice of an effective dialogical paradigm in dialogue between the two religions in Nigeria.

In Christian theology of religions, there have been different typologies proposed by theologians to classify Christians' approach to dialogue with other religions. However, the tripod paradigm of exclusivism, pluralism and inclusivism by Alan Race has dominated theological discussion and is suitable in explicating the trend in the Nigerian context. This book posits inclusivism by countering the approaches of exclusivism and pluralism. Exclusivism makes the claim for revelation and salvation only through Jesus Christ. Those in other religions are to be converted and to make explicit profession of faith in Christianity, without which they face the likely consequence of losing salvation. This approach makes dialogue impossible because it is difficult to balance this view with God's universal love for all people, since people's religions emerges from their cultural context. Pluralism opposes this stance by considering every religion as a valid path to the ultimate reality. John Hick created an ineffable Real to which all religions are united, while Knitter finds the unity of all religions in the effort to overcome common human sufferings, injustices and the preservation of the ecosystem. The problem with the former is that it fails to recognize that religions ask different questions and are guided towards different ultimate ends. The latter neglects the fact that ethical judgements are based on *a priori* principles and transcendental beliefs of religions. However, inclusivism falls in-between the two extremities. While acknowledging God's universal love for all people (a possibility for salvation), it maintains that this love is made particularly in Jesus Christ. There is salvific optimism for people of other religions, but this is made possible by Jesus Christ.

This resonates with the Post-Vatican II position of the Roman Catholic Church. The Second Vatican Council acknowledges elements of "truth" and "goodness "and "seed of the word" in the religions of the world. They are however, seen as rays of light, that will be brought to the fullness of light in Christianity. In this view, Karl Rahner describes people from other religions who have not explicitly professed faith in Jesus but live a life of truth and love, as anonymous Christians. It means that they have implicit faith. Inclusivism received more hermeneutical analysis by two contemporary theologians: Dupuis and D'Costa. Both proceeded from Trinitarian Theology to assign Jesus not an absolute role in relation to salvation, but a constitutive-relational and normative role respectively. For Dupuis, Jesus is Truly but not the Only savior. For D'Costa, Jesus is wholly God and not the whole of God. The Spirit's activity among the religions is given special consideration and interpretation. For D'Costa, If Christianity is to be faithful to its calling, it must listen to what the Spirit reveals in other religions. Dupuis considers the incarnation as significant but limits the activity of Jesus, the God-man. The Spirit or Logos which has been there at creation can bring salvation to those outsides of Christianity. This is made possible by the significant intervention of Christ in human history.

Similarly, in Islam we find some elements that form analogous interpretation of commonality for an inclusive relationship. A look at the teachings of two Islamic scholars, reveal greater potentials for openness to the people of the book. The interpretation of *Rahma* as one of the attributes of *Allah*, describes as encompassing God's mercy and love, and resonates with the fundamental Christian teachings on love of God and neighbor. Love of God and neighbor forms important inclusive category for dialogue between Muslims and Christians.

Inclusivism is criticized for its imperialist and triumphalist posture. Interpreting other religions with Christian categories and finding them fulfilled in Christianity without according them the possibility of salvation on their own terms poses a significant obstacle for effective dialogue. Nevertheless,

Inclusivism overcomes two extremes: of excluding other religions from salvation and the unification of religions under a philosophical or ethical ground that neglect the irreducible particularity of individual religions. It embraces openness, commitment to dialogue, respect and love for other religions. And like pluralism, inclusivism is open to joint initiatives and working together to overcome common human problems. As a paradigm of interreligious dialogue, these principles make inclusivism better suited in the dialogue between Christians and Muslims. Inclusivism fulfills the condition of the four forms of dialogue mentioned in the previous chapter.

The application and contextualization of inclusivism through the four forms of dialogue, portrays how effective it could function in achieving peaceful co-existence between Christians and Muslims in Nigeria. Although we located inclusive categories in play in the dialogue of theological exchange and the dialogue of spiritual experience, this book argues that it is more *ad rem* in the praxis of dialogue of life and the dialogue of action. These two forms of dialogue are described as social dialogues. Dialogue of life and action engages in the daily realities of peoples' encounters and challenges in their society. The socio-economic and political challenges facing Nigerians are in most cases, the root causes of the religious conflicts. These challenges find appropriate theological response in the praxis of the inclusive categories of love, forgiveness, compassion and mercy that are taught in both religions. Social dialogues are posited as effective in the Nigeria context because of their practical engagement in the daily life and challenges of members of both religions in the Nigeria context, they, however, correlate with dialogue of theological exchange as the necessary foundation. In summation, this book makes the case that proper understanding and interpretations of inclusivism, form a foundation for the praxis of effective dialogical engagement and peaceful coexistence between Christians and Muslims in the Nigerian context.

Bibliography

Achebe, Chinua. *There was a Country.* New York, Penguin Press, 2012.

Akinade, Akintunde. *Christian Response to Islam in Nigeria: A Contextual Study of Ambivalent Encounters. New York: Palgrave Macmillan, 2014.*

Arinze, Cardinal Francis. *Meeting other Believers: The Risks and Rewards of Interreligious Dialogue. Huntington, Indiana: Our Sunday Visitor Publishing Division, 1998.*

Arnold, Thomas Walker. *The Preaching of Islam; A History of the Propagation of the Muslim Faith. London: Luzac& Company, 1935.*

Ayegboyin, Deji and Ishola, S. Ademola. *African Indigenous Churches: An Historical Perspective.* Lagos, Nigeria: Greater Heights Publications, 1999.

Barth, Karl. "The Revelation of God as the Abolition of Religion," *Christianity and other Religions; Selected Readings.* eds. John Hick and Brian Hebblethwaite. Oxford: Becker, Karl Joseph and Morali, Ilaria. *Catholic Engagement with World Religions: A Comprehensive Study.* Maryknoll, N.Y.: Orbis Books, 2010.

Bevans, Stephen B., and Roger Schroeder. Constants in Context: A Theology of Mission for Today. Maryknoll, N.Y.: Orbis Books, 2004.

Bormans, Maurice. *Guidelines for Dialogue between Christians and Muslims.* New York: Paulist Press, 1990.

Brunner, Emil. "Nature and Grace." *Natural Theology*. eds. Emil Brunner and Karl Barth, trans. Peter Fraenkel. London, UK: Geoffrey Bles, 1946.

Bujo, Bénézet, *African Theology in its Social Context*. Maryknoll, NY: Orbis Books, 1992.

Comolli, Virginia. *Boko Haram: Nigeria's Islamist Insurgency*. London: Hurt and Company, 2015.

Cornille, Catherine. *The Im-possibility of Interreligious Dialogue*. New York: The Crossroad Publishing Company, 2008.

____________, and Christopher Conway. *Interreligious Hermeneutics*. Eugene, Or: Cascade Books, 2010.

____________, and ValereNeckebrouck. *A Universal Faith? Peoples, Cultures, Religions, and the Christ: Essays in Honor of Prof. Dr. Frank De Graeve*. Louvain: Peeters Press, 1992.

D'Costa, Gavin. *Christian Uniqueness Reconsidered: The Myth of a Pluralistic Theology of Religions*. Maryknoll, N.Y.: Orbis Books, 1990.

____________. *The Meeting of the Religions and the Trinity*. Edinburgh: T & T Clark, 2000.

____________. *The Catholic Church and the World Religions: A Theological and Phenomenological Account*. London: T & T Clark, 2011.

Dupuis, Jacques. *Christianity and the Religions: From Confrontation to Dialogue.* Maryknoll, N.Y.: Orbis Books, 2002.

__________. *Towards a Christian Theology of Religious Pluralism.* Maryknoll: Orbis Books, 1997.

__________, and Josef Neuner. *The Christian Faith in the Doctrinal Documents of the Catholic Church.* New York: Alba House, 2001.

__________, and William R. Burrows. *Jacques Dupuis Faces the Inquisition: Two Essays by Jacques Dupuis on Dominus Iesus and the Roman Investigation of His Work.* Eugene, Or: Pickwick Publications, 2012.

Falola, Toyin, *Colonialism and Violence in Nigeria.* Bloomington and Indianapolis: IN: University Press, 2009.

__________. *The History of Nigeria.* Westport, Conn: Greenwood Press, 1999.

Fitzgerald, Allan, and John C. Cavadini. *Augustine Through the Ages: An Encyclopedia.* Grand Rapids, Mich: W.B. Eerdmans, 1999.

Flannery, Austin.*The Basic Sixteen Documents: Vatican Council II Constitutions Decrees Declarations.* Northport, New York: Costello Publishing Company, 1996.

Hallencreutz, Carl F. *New Approaches to Men of Other Faiths.* WCC, Geneva 1970.

Harris, J. Elizabeth, Hedges, Paul and Hettiarachchi, Shanthikumar. *Twenty-First Century Theologies of Religions: Retrospection and Future.* Leiden, Boston: Brill-Rodopi, 2016.

Hatch, John. *Nigeria: A History.* London: Secker and Warburg, 1970.

Hedges, Paul. "Reflection on Typologies: Negotiating a Fast-Moving Discussion," *Christian Approaches to Other Faiths. eds. Alan Race and Paul Hedges.* London: SCM, 2008.

Heim, S. Mark. *Is Christ the Only Way?: Christian Faith in a Pluralistic World.* Valley Forge, PA: Judson Press, 1985.

__________. *Salvations: Truth and Difference in Religion.* Maryknoll, N.Y.: Orbis Books, 1995.

Hick, John. *A Christian Theology of Religions.* Louisville: Westminster John Knox Press, 1995.

__________.*An Interpretation of Religion.* Basingstoke: MacMillan, 1989.

__________. *God and the Universe of Faiths.* New York: St. Martin's Press, 1973.

__________, and Brian Hebblethwaite. *Christianity and Other Religions: Selected Readings.* Oxford: Oneworld, 2001.

__________, and Paul F. Knitter. *The Myth of Christian Uniqueness: Toward a Pluralistic Theology of Religions*. Maryknoll, N.Y.: Orbis Books, 1987.

Hussain, Amir. *Oil and Water: Two Faiths: One God*. Kelowna, BC: CopperHouse, 2006.

Iweala, Okonjo Ngozi. *Reforming the Unreformable: Lessons from Nigeria*. Cambridge, MA: MIT Press, 2012.

Iwuchkwu, Marinus, *Muslim-Christian Dialogue in Postcolonial Northern Nigeria: The Challenges of Inclusive Cultural and Religious Pluralism*. New York: Palgrave Macmillan, 2013.

Kane, Ousmane. *Muslim Modernity in Postcolonial Nigeria: A Study of the Society for the Removal of Innovation and Reinstatement of Tradition*. Leiden: Bill, 2003.

Kärkkäinen, Veli-Matti. *Trinity and Religious Pluralism: The Doctrine of the Trinity in Christian Theology of Religions*. Aldershot, Hants, England: Ashgate, 2004.

Kenny, Joseph. "Christian-Muslim Relations in Nigeria," *Christianity and Islam: The struggling Dialogue, ed., Richard W. Rousseau*. Montrose, Ridge & Row Press, 1985.

Kirk, Andrew J. *What is Mission? Theological Exploration*. Minneapolis: Fortress Press, 2000.

Knitter, Paul F. *Introducing Theologies of Religions*. Maryknoll, NY: Orbis Books, 2002.

__________. *One Earth, Many Religions: Multifaith Dialogue and Global Responsibility*. Maryknoll, N.Y.: Orbis Books, 1995.

Kraemer, Hendrick. *The Christian Message in a Non-Christian World*. Grand Rapids, MI: Kregel Publication, 1956.

McGrath, Alister E. *The Open Secret: A New Vision for Natural Theology*. Malden, MA: Blackwell, 2008.

Mohammed, Ovey N. *Muslim-Christian Relations: Past, Present, Future*. Maryknoll, NY: Orbis Books, 1999.

Moyaert, Marianne. *In Response to the Religious Other: Ricoeur and the Fragility of Interreligious Encounters*. Lanham, MD: Lexington Books, 2014.

Netland, Harold A. *Dissonant Voices: Religious Pluralism and the Question of Truth*. Grand Rapids, Mich: W.B. Eerdmans, 1991.

Newbigin, Lesslie. *The Open Secret: Sketches for a Missionary Theology*. Grand Rapids:Eerdmans, 1978.

Onibere, S. G. A., and Michael P. Adogbo. *Selected Themes in the Study of Religions in Nigeria*. Surulere, Lagos: Malthouse, 2010.

Pope, Stephen J., and Charles Hefling. *Sic Et Non: Encountering Dominus Iesus*. 2002.

Race, Alan. *Christians and Religious Pluralism: Patterns in the Christian Theology of Religions*. Maryknoll, NY: Orbis Books, 1982.

Rahner, Karl. *Theological Investigations*. London: Darton, Longman & Todd, 1961.

Ruthven, Malise. *Fundamentalism: A Very Short Introduction*. Oxford: Oxford University Press, 2007.

Salihu, J. *Interreligious Dialogue and Sharia*. Kano, Nigeria: Jalejemi Group, 2005.

Schineller, Peter. *Pastoral Letters and Communiqués of the Catholic Bishops' Conference of Nigeria, 1960-2002: The Voice of the Voiceless*. Abuja, Nigeria: Gaudium Et Spes Institute, 2002.

Sharpe, Eric J. *Faith Meets Faith*. SCM Press, London 1977.

Shah-Kazemi, Reza. *My Mercy Encompasses All: The Koran's Teachings on Compassion, Peace & Love*. Emeryville, California: Shoemaker & Hoard, 2007.

__________. *The Other in the Light of the One: The Universality of the Qur'ān and Interfaith Dialogue*. Cambridge [England]: Islamic Texts Society, 2006.

__________. *The Spirit of Tolerance in Islam*. London: I.B. Tauris in association with the Institute of Ismaili Studies, 2012.

Smith, Wilfred Cantwell. *Towards a World Theology: Faith and the Comparative History of Religion*. Philadelphia, Pa: Westminster Press, 1981.

Teasdale, Wayne. *Catholicism in Dialogue: Conversations Across Traditions*. Lanham, Md: Rowman & Littlefield Publishers, 2004.

Volf, Miroslav, Ghazi bin Muhammad, and Melissa Yarrington. *A Common Word: Muslims and Christians on Loving God and Neighbor*. Grand Rapids, Mich: W.B. Eerdmans Pub. Co, 2010.

Vorgrimler, Herbert. *Commentary on the documents of Vatican II*. New York: Herder and Herder, 1967.

Thomas, Owen C. *Attitudes Towards Other Religions*. London: SCM Press, 1969.

Tilley, Terrence W. *Religious Diversity and the American Experience: A Theological Approach*. New York: Continuum, 2007.

Documents and Journal Articles

Alao, Olatunji E. and Mavalla, Ayuba G. "Kaduna State Sharia Crisis of 2000: The Lessons and Challenges after Sixteen Years." *Journal of Humanities and Social Science* 21, no. 10 (October 2016):8-14.

Building Bridges Seminar, Mosher, Lucinda, and David Marshall. *Sin, Forgiveness, and Reconciliation: Christian and Muslim Perspectives*: A Record of the Thirteenth Building Bridges Seminar Hosted by Georgetown University Washington, District of Columbia & Warrenton, Virginia (April 27 – 30, 2016).

Catholic Bishops' Conference of Nigeria. "While Nigeria Bleeds and Burns."September 18, 2014. Accessed June 8, 2017. http://www.cbcn-ng.org/.

Catholic Church. *Catechism of the Catholic Church: With Modifications from the Editio Typica.* Toronto: Image Book Doubleday, 1995.

__________. "Declaration on Religious Liberty." *The Basic Sixteen Documents:*

*Vatican Council II Constitutions Decrees Declarations, ed., Austin Flannery.*Northport, New York: Costello Publishing Company, 1996.

__________. "Dogmatic Constitution on the Church" - *Lumen Gentium.* AccessedApril 30, 2017. http://www.vatican.va/archive/hist_councils/ii_vatican_council/documents/vat-ii_const_19641121_lumen-gentium_en.html

__________. "Degree on the Mission Activity of the Church" – *Ad Gentes.* Accessed April 30, 2017 http://www.vatican.va/archive/hist_councils/ii_vatican_council/documents/vat-ii_decree_19651207_ad-gentes_en.html.

__________. "Pastoral Constitution on the Church in the Modern World" – *Gauduim et Spes.* Accessed April 30, 2017. http://www.vatican.va/archive/hist_councils/ii_vatican_council/documents/vat-ii_cons_19651207_gaudium-et-spes_en.html.

Congregation for the Doctrine of Faith. *Dominus Iesus: On the Unicity and Salvific*

Universality of Jesus Christ and the Church. Accessed May 21, 2017.
http://www.vatican.va/roman_curia/congregations/cfait h/documents/rc_con_cfaith_doc_20000806_dominus-iesus_en.html.

__________. "Notification on the book Towards a Christian Theology of Religious Pluralism by Fr. Jacques Dupuis." Accessed May 21, 2017. http://www.vatican.va/roman_curia/congregations/cfait h/documents/rc_con_cfaith_doc_20010124_dupuis_en. html.

D'Costa, Gavin. "A Christian Reflection on Some Problems with Discerning 'God' in the World Religions," *Dialogue and Alliance 5* (1991):4 - 17.

__________. "Karl Rahner Anonymous Christian – A Reappraisal," *Modern Theology* 1 no.2 (January 1985): 131-148.

__________. "Revelation and Revelations: Discerning God in Other Religions. Beyond a Static Valuation," *Modern Theology* 10, no.2 (1994): 165 - 183.

__________. "The Holy Spirit and the World Religions," *Louvain Studies* 34 (2010): 279-311.

Dias, Darren J. "Fifty Years and the Learning: Development in the Roman Catholic Church's Encounter with Religions." *Toronto Journal of Theology* 32, no.2 (Fall 2016): 341 – 361.

Drake, H.A. "Intolerance, Religious Violence, and Political Legitimacy in Late Antiquity." *Journal of the American Academy of Religion* 79, no. 1 (2011): 193-235.

Fitzgerald, Michael L. "Christian Muslim Dialogue: A Survey of Recent Developments." (2000). Accessed July 1, 2017. www.sedos.org/english/fitzgerald.htm.

Hick, John. "The Possibility of Religious Pluralism: A Response to Gavin D'Costa." *Religious Studies* 33, no.2 (June 1997): 166-166.

Hussain, Amir. "From Tolerance to Dialogue: A Muslim Perspective on Interfaith Dialogue with Christians." *Asian Christian Review* 2 no. 2&3 (Summer/Winter2008): 85 - 97.

Litonjua, M.D. "Religious Zealotry and Political Violence in Christianity and Islam." *International Review of Modern Sociology* 35, no.2 (2009), 307-331.

Knitter, Paul F. "Catholics and Other Religions: Bridging the Gap Between Dialogue and Theology." *Louvain Studies* 24 (1999): 319-354.

Koehler, Daniel. "Right-Wing Extremism and Terrorism in Europe: Current Development and Issues for the Future." *Prism: A Journal of the Center for Complex Operations* 6, no. 2 (July 2016), 84-104.

__________. "Making Sense of the Many," *Religious Studies Review* 15, no.3 (July 1989): 204-207.

Mamodu, Umar. "Boko Haram – the Beginning" *Boko Haram: How a Militant Islamist Group Emerged in Nigeria*, ed. Femi Owolade. Accessed November. 24, 2016.

http://www.gatestoneinstitute.org/4232/boko-haram-nigeria#_ftnref1.

Muck, Terry. "Instrumentality, Complexity, and Reason: A Christian Approach to Religions," *Buddhist-Christian Studies* 22 (2002): 115 - 121.

O'Collins, Gerald. "Jacques Dupuis Contributions to Interreligious Dialogue." *Theological Studies* 64, (2003): 388 - 397.

__________. "John Paul II on Christ, the Holy Spirit, and World Religions." *Irish Theological Quarterly* 72 (November 2007): 323 - 337.

Onaiyekan, John. "The sharia in Nigeria: A Christian View." *Bulletin on Islam and Christian-Muslim Relations in Africa* 5, no.3 (1987): 1 - 17.

Pope Benedict XVI, Deus Caritas Est. Accessed December 6, 2017. http://w2.vatican.va/content/benedict-xvi/en/encyclicals/documents/hf_ben-xvi_enc_20051225_deus-caritas-est.html.

__________. Africa Munus - Post-Synodal Apostolic Exhortation; Accessed, June 27, 2017. http://w2.vatican.va/content/benedict-xvi/en/apost_exhortations/documents/hf_ben-xvi_exh_20111119_africae-munus.html.

Pope Paul VI. "EvangeliiNuntiandi - Apostolic Exhortation."
Accessed December 20, 2017.
http://w2.vatican.va/content/paul-
vi/en/apost_exhortations/documents/hf_p-
vi_exh_19751208_evangelii-nuntiandi.html.

Pope Francis. *Evangelii Gaudium.* Accessed December 11,
2017.
http://w2.vatican.va/content/francesco/en/apost_exhorta
tions/documents/papa-francesco_esortazione-
ap_20131124_evangelii-gaudium.html.

Pope John Paul II. Address to Young Muslims inMorocco.
Monday, 19 August 1985. Accessed, Jan. 12, 2018.
http://w2.vatican.va/content/john-paul-
ii/en/speeches/1985/august/documents/hf_jp-
ii_spe_19850819_giovani-stadio-casablanca.html.

___________. "Dominum et Vivificantem: On the Holy Spirit
in the Life of the Church and the World." Accessed
December 21, 2017. http://w2.vatican.va/content/john-
paul-ii/en/encyclicals/documents/hf_jp-
ii_enc_18051986_dominum-et-vivificantem.html.

___________. *Ecclesia in Africa* - Post-Synodal Apostolic
Exhortation. Accessed December 8, 2017.
http://w2.vatican.va/content/john-
paulii/en/apost_exhortations/documents/hf_jpii_exh_14
091995_ecclesia-in-africa.html.

___________. "RedemptorisMissio: On the Permanent
Validity of the Church's Missionary Mandate."
Accessed December 21, 2017.

http://w2.vatican.va/content/john-paul-
ii/en/encyclicals/documents/hf_jp-
ii_enc_07121990_redemptoris-missio.html.

____________. "Redemptor Hominis: An Encyclical letter."
Accessed December 21, 2016.
http://w2.vatican.va/content/john-paul-
ii/en/encyclicals/documents/hf_jp-
ii_enc_04031979_redemptor-hominis.html.

Ratzinger, Cardinal Joseph. "Relativism: The Central Problem
for Faith Today." Accessed April 12, 2017.
http://www.ewtn.com/library/CURIA/RATZRELA.htm
.

Reynolds, Thomas. "Theology and Religious Others: The
Unity of Love of God and Neighbor and Interreligious
Hermeneutics." *Science et Espirit* 68, no.2&3 (2016):
257-274.

Sampson, Isaac T. "Religious Violence in Nigeria: Causal
Diagnoses and Strategic Recommendation to the State
Religious Communities" *African Centre for the
Constructive Resolution of Disputes. Accessed Feb. 6,
2017.*

http://www.accord.org.za/ajcr-
issues/%EF%BF%BCreligious-violence-in-nigeria/.

Schineller, Peter J. "Christ and Church: A Spectrum of
Views," *Theological Studies* 37 no. 4. December 1976,
545-566.

Sule, Maijama'a. "Remembering Mallam Aminu Kano." *Premium Times* (June 19, 2017). Accessed, June 20, 2017. http://www.premiumtimesng.com/opinion/5163-remembering_mallam_aminu_kano.html.

Uhrmacher, Kevin and Sheridan, Mary B. "The Brutal Tool of Boko Haram's Attacks on Civilians," *The Washington Post*, April 3, 2016. Accessed March 9, 2017. https://www.washingtonpost.com/graphics/world/nigeria-boko-haram/.

Ukaonu, Ambrose Eze, "Developing an Islamo-Christian Theology of Love for an Effective Inter-Religious Dialogue in Nigeria," *Journal of Inculturation Theology* 13, no.2, (2012): 152-166.

Wing, Ng Kam. "Pluralism and Particularity of Salvation in Christ," *Krisis and Praxis* (2006). Accessed, May 3, 2017. http://www.krisispraxis.com.

Tanebuam's Peacemakers in Action. "Imam Muhammad and Pastor James Wuye." Accessed December 9, 2017. https://tanenbaum.org/peacemakers-in-action-network/meet-the-peacemakers/imam-muhammad-ashafa-pastor-james-wuye/.

The Secretariat for Non-Christian, "The Attitude of the Church to the Followers of other Religions: Reflections and Orientations on Dialogue and Mission." Accessed, January12,2018.http://www.fabriceblee.com/uploads/3/1/6/5/3165415/dialogue_and_mission_eng.pdf.